THE PATH THROUGH
THE LABYRINTH

The Quest for Initiation
into the Western Mystery Tradition

Marian Green

D1437523

Marian Green has been the Editor of *Quest* quarterly magazine since 1970. This journal contains a variety of articles on all aspects of the Western Mystery Tradition, natural magic, divination and personal magical experiences, as well as book reviews and news of conferences and events.

Marian also runs several correspondence courses on Ceremonial and Natural Magic, holds workshops, and gives talks and practical training to small groups throughout Britain and Europe.

Full details of her courses and cassettes are available from *BCM - SCL Quest, London WC1N 3XX*. Please enclose a large stamped, self-addressed envelope.

THE PATH THROUGH
THE LABYRINTH

The Quest for Initiation
into the Western Mystery Tradition

Marian Green

E L E M E N T   B O O K S

First published 1988 by
Element Books Limited
Longmead, Shaftesbury, Dorset

Printed and bound in Great Britain by
Billings, Hylton Road, Worcester

Cover illustration by Courtney Davis

Design by Max Fairbrother

British Library Cataloguing in Publication Data
Green, Marian
The path through the labyrinth: the quest
for initiation into the western mystery
tradition.
1. Occult practices. Initiation
I. Title
133

ISBN 1-85230-034-5

Contents

This book is dedicated to the memory of my Father.
His quiet wisdom and gentle humour will be long missed.
W. G. S. Live in the Light.

Introduction

THE WAY IN – A NOVICE'S CATCH 22

Not this; not that. History traces two paths to the Truth. This is called
science. That is called religion. … They assume it has to be this and
that and nothing besides, science and religion distinct forever. Valid –
one or other or both – as the only roads there are. As the highways
through a wilderness where all else is trackless fancy and superstition.
For us here and now, however, I say: *not* this, *not* that.

Geoffrey Ashe, The Finger and the Moon

Books, cassette tapes, Tarot packs, Rune cards, crystal balls,
aura goggles, astrological data discs, and yet more books – where
on earth should the Seeker begin his path to wisdom? At every
turn he is hemmed in, on the one side by the intriguing possibilities of *magic*, and on the other by his own limited knowledge and
experience. On one hand there is the desire to explore, try out and
master the arcane arts, and on the other hand there is his natural
fear of the unknown, and often unknowable. This is the Novice's
Catch 22. If he plunges straight into a study of the first subject he
encounters he might run into unnamed dangers; if he hangs back,

relying on reason and caution, he will never experience the reality of the magical universe. He stands alone, unguided at the very door of the Mysteries, yet may very well hesitate before plunging into the mapless maze which he so desires to explore. This is not lack of wisdom, nor are his fears entirely groundless.

The occult world is a strange place until you learn its hidden paths, understand its symbolism and feel safe walking within its ever-changing bounds, but these things only come with practice and consistent effort. The journey within takes the Seeker into the secret depths of his own being, totally cut off from guidance, and usually completely unexplored in ordinary life, and if he is experiencing the effects of even the most basic magical experiment he may well be frightened and surprised at what happens to him.

Most books explain precisely *how* to perform the basic exercises, very few give more than a brief mention of *what happens*, *why it happens* and *what* the novice should expect to feel, see, discover. Certainly people's actual experiences vary from individual to individual, but there are shared patterns, common to most who make a serious attempt at relearning these ancient skills and techniques. It is true that you cannot really understand what is happening to you unless you have been through it before, and in magic much of the work involves experiment and stretching beyond the known limits. It is a very confusing world, for it also has different rules to the ordinary world. Magicians talk easily about past lives, of travelling through time and space, in 'the astral', of invoking angels and receiving instruction directly from goddesses or gods, of using symbols to make talismans which will protect or attract what they seek. This is all very fascinating and intriguing to the Seeker, but it is hard for him to know that there is a middle way which twists and turns right through the labyrinth to the great goal in the centre. To show him that safe path is the main objective of this book.

What I am trying to do is to explain what might be encountered at the various junctions on the path. Where there is a choice of turning right or left, or of going straight ahead, rather than saying 'Turn left' I will attempt to explain what might be discovered in each direction, what might be gained, and when it is better to leave that passage to another time, for it must be the Seeker's own choice of path which he takes. The maze has solid sides, built stone by stone of ancient wisdom; strange, mind-awakening techniques; great slabs of symbolism and mythology, and high walls of knowledge which have to be explained and remembered. It is so often the case that if you knew the answer you wouldn't need to ask the oracle, or perform the ritual, and in magic you often don't even know what the question is!

There are three 'P's which are vital to magical achievement: Patience, Perseverance and Practice. You cannot master the wisdom of thousands of years instantly, no matter what some book or video might suggest, any more than you can play the oboe or guitar after only one lesson. You will need to read, to study and to fill up the shelves in your own data store with masses of information, and persevere with some dull and even boring exercises until you can do them without effort and thought. Unless you lay down those foundation techniques you will become utterly lost in the Inner Worlds, because you will not even be able to recognise the way out. Practice *does* make perfect, and just as with mastering a musical instrument, learning another language or gaining a skill in handicrafts, you just have to keep at it. If you do it right, however, even the basic exercises become interesting, for they open new vistas through the labyrinth, and you start to see the path before you.

The path I am trying to map out for new Seekers is that of the Western Mystery Tradition. Many people living in Britain and America have had to seek guidance from the Masters of the East because those teachings were most readily available and common, whereas the arts and magic of the Western Tradition had remained shrouded in obscurity and mystification. Now the tide is flowing a little in the opposite direction. Most of the traditional arts, many of which in the West rely upon story-telling and imagination rather than repeated mantras and chants, are being clarified and made available to us. The hardest thing to convey about them is their basic simplicity and directness. Many Seekers are astounded that the basic arts of meditation and creative visualisation can be so powerful, and instead of settling down to months of steady practice to master these vital skills, they turn away, looking for greater mysteries, more elaborate techniques, more exotic practices.

Anyone who seeks, with an honest heart and a bit of persistence and dedication, can find a way through the labyrinth to the inner mystery wherein his or her own uniqueness, individuality and inborn talents for healing, for love and for respect can be fully developed. Part of the journey is difficult, some of it will raise doubts and cause the Seeker to confront faults and failings;

much of it is lonely, for the path to the heart is essentially a solo one, but it will be filled with adventure, with joy brought forth from self-confidence. There will be fun and laughter as well as tears and disappointments. In the end, those sturdy souls who reach the convergence of all true paths will discover spiritual treasures beyond their wildest dreams. Each of us inherits many powers, links with our eternal and all-knowing selves, but life and mundane matters have built walls which shut off these immanent sources of wisdom and fulfilment. We do not see our own attainable perfection because no one has told us it is there to see, nor felt the inexhaustible forces of the universe which are there at our command because it isn't included in a normal school curriculum. I say to you now, 'You are unique, your life is valuable, and you can learn to shape Creation to bring health, to bring joy and to bring fulfilment, if you follow the path of your spirit, as it wanders through the tangle of life's lessons. Within you are the seeds of greatness, and only you can release them; nurture them that they may flower and fruit for the benefit of the whole universe.' The exercises, the considerations and the ideas in this book are not the only way; there are as many paths through life as there are those who will follow them, but if you are wandering lost then any map will be a little help, and from it you may find your own true path.

EXPLANATION

The Path through the Labyrinth is about the Quest for Initiation into the Western Mystery Tradition. Many people are well aware of the mystical, philosophical and religious systems of the East, for in those lands and cultures the national religion has walked hand in hand with its mystical, magical and spiritual traditions. In the West, in Europe, Britain and Ireland, the state religion has held its own Mysteries secretly, revealing them only to the ordained priesthood, not all of whom, over the last nineteen centuries have either understood or been able to function with the power such knowledge brings with it. Therefore it has been necessary to conceal the inner, spiritual way, the way of the soul rather than that of the body. Circumstances have made it impossible for there to be continuous secret schools; wars and crusades have taken away those with knowledge, yet underlying the fragmentation and control of the people, the Western

Mystery Tradition has survived, been enhanced, and is now ready to flower again in the world.

The ways in which the actual spiritual values and traditional rites of worship have survived the vicissitudes of the world have been several in number. On the one hand, in Britain and Europe there is a strong and enduring folk tradition, of songs and tales, legends and public celebrations, festivals and seasonal gatherings during which the stories of the Old Gods, who have never entirely faded from consciousness, are welcomed and worshipped, their stories retold and relived by all the participants. The magical arts, those of divination, of healing and of personal questing for the eternal have also been preserved at a very simple, almost trivial, level by the Wise Women, the Cunning Men, the healer, the witch, the herbalist and the Horse Doctor. Another deeper level has been nurtured by the scholars, writing secretly through the ages, even when their lands were at war, and studying the stars, and the stones, the lives of animals and mankind, and the working of God throughout the known universe. From these hidden literary stores and their students have come the arts of astronomy and astrology, alchemy and the physical sciences, many practical healing arts including that study of the soul, psychology and psychiatry. From the Holy Land via Spain has come the wisdom of Qabalah, the Jewish philosophical system which gives a firm structure to the understanding of Creation in all its manifestations, and a symbolic language in which it might be discussed and shared with others, open to that knowledge.

A later manifestation which captured and held (and still holds) the collective imagination is that of the Legend of the Holy Grail, the Quest for that archetypal 'something' which has the power to heal the world, adjust the entire system so that all have their needs fulfilled, which will make green anew the Wasteland, whether laid waste by war or man or nuclear disaster.

We have always sought answers to the eternal questions about life, and the universe, and the place of mankind in Creation, and for many years, since book learning, international travel and interchange of ideas have brought about greater contacts with other traditions and other philosophies, many students have been able to discover in the East those things which have become totally hidden and apparently lost in the West. But now the rose is being allowed to bloom again in the wilderness, for those who go forth to be gardeners of the spirit have found it, pruned it back, and cut away the overgrowing jungle of orthodoxy and enforced religious belief. Underneath these strangling vines the Light of Knowledge has penetrated and in the darkness the bright blossoms of our own tradition are being allowed to put forth their faces into the light of day, to take their place beside the Eastern Lotus.

Although there has been a long scholarly tradition in Europe and Britain, the folklore and its powerful mysteries have been preserved within the oral, rather than the literary, heritage of the land. We still have the folk-songs, the ballads, the legends, the heroic tales which were current before the Romans came to Britain two thousand years ago! We have the ancient inheritance of the Druids passed on by word and action, by story and song, kept sacred among the uneducated ordinary folk to whom the written word, the printed book and the dead record of ink on paper were strange manifestations of some alien culture. We have been happy to bask in the Light which came from the East and have forgotten to look for the Light that shines in the West, but now that Light is being seen and recognised. Underneath the Christian facade there has been an ongoing pagan stream, running fresh from its source, overlooked by the learned, but still tasted and known to be pure by the country folk, the village healers, the magicians and those who work with the power of Nature to restore the world. There have always been secret fellowships who have sought out this eternal spring of Western wisdom and who have kept the sacred ways for thousands of years, each preserving a few ancient threads of the great pattern, and now it is time for those shining strands to be rewoven into a tapestry which may be seen by all and understood by those who have the keys to the Mysteries.

There are clear patterns to follow by ritually re-enacting the tasks of the Heroes, there are festivals which celebrate the sacredness of Nature and the turning seasons of the year, there are many clues which can lead the modern, urbanised, denatured individual on a journey of self-exploration so that he may recover the gifts of the spirit, and rescue the eternal from the mundane. It is a long and lonely path, for just as the Eastern initiate has to seek out a teacher in the high and remote mountains, so does the Western wanderer have to find his instructor within the wilderness where only the forces of Nature can initiate him and restore his true path within Creation.

Now he does not journey unprepared, for a few wise and daring scholars of our Native Tradition have written guidebooks: Christine Hartley *The Western Mystery Tradition* in 1968, Lewis Spence *The Mysteries of Britain* in the 1920s, John and Caitlin Matthews their valuable contemporary study in two volumes, *The Western Way*, and Caitlin Matthews *Mabon and the Mysteries of Britain*. Bob Stewart has explored this oral magical tradition using the life of the Magician/Prophet Merlin in *The Mystic Life of Merlin* and *The Prophetic Vision of Merlin* and his earlier book, *The Underworld Initiation*, in each case drawing on very early literary sources which were the last incarnation of a much more ancient oral tradition.

Each of these important books sets out aspects of the history, the wealth of knowledge, the ancientness and validity of the Western Mystery Tradition and each will lead the wanderer further along the path to self-awareness and experience of his native tradition, but it is not the complete story.

In our civilised and settled Western world where the mundane is catered for, and most have at least the necessities of life, there is an unexplored spiritual dimension which orthodox religion no longer seems to address, and the material system of acquiring 'things' does not understand at all. It is here that people look for fulfilment of an inner longing and do not know where to turn for guidance. Looking to the East they have seen that there are gurus and teachers who have led their followers to a deeper understanding and new philosophy, but that doesn't appeal to all who now recognise their need for spiritual instruction. The Western Tradition has always been that of a Quest, an individual journey through the apparent world wherein the lessons are learned at an inner level, and it is the spirit which is nourished. To travel alone shows that there can be no handy teacher, no companion class within a school, no learned tutor from whom ongoing instruction can be sought. It is possible only to take those personal resources, that initial knowledge gained from books or from the experiences of life to guide and assist along the winding path of the Western Way to Self-Initiation which is true self-knowledge and power. Each person's Quest will be individual, his or her goal personal, his or her path straight or convoluted, clear or overgrown as each finds it, but many common things will be encountered along the way, many experiences shared, many similar way-marks seen and understood. That is what this text is about – those points on the map of this inner journey which will guide most travellers on the road to true happiness and perfect peace. It will show them how to read the old tales and see them as texts describing accurately the Path of the Initiate, to see in the shifting patterns of stars and seasons those things which are eternal – to find within themselves the ultimate keys of the Mysteries of the West.

One of the essential factors is that the initiate, be he bard, poet, priest of the pagan ways, shaman, witch or any other Seeker of the Western Mysteries must be bonded to the Earth. From the earliest time in our history the magicians, the priests and the people have shaped the earth, raising up stone circles and ellipses, constructing banks and ditches, marking out the confines of sacred areas, and setting natural stone or tree markers in that place. Some of those which are still visible in Britain and Europe are six or seven thousand years old. The trainee or the individual, driven by inner forces, had to go alone to a sacred place, be it hilltop, or spring, cave or sea-shore, and there he would meet with the initiator, perhaps seen as the Goddess of the Earth. Later, where natural caves were not present, as they don't occur in chalk or clay landscapes, mounds lined with stones were set up. It was within these earthy chambers that the initiate made his bond to the Earth, and the Underworld and there received the keys of vision, poetic inspiration, magical power, healing and all the other things which any true initiate is capable of. Even kings and queens to this day are crowned in England on the 'Coronation Stone' from Scone in Scotland.

In legend Merlin the Magician ran wild in the forest until he was cured of his madness by musical inspiration. King Arthur had to enter and bring back from Annwn, the Welsh Underworld, pigs and the Cauldron of Rebirth. Demeter sought the Kore in the Underworld and found her daughter changed by becoming Pluto's bride and Queen of the Underworld, ruling the dead and the unborn for half the year. In each case a close contact with elemental Earth or Mother Nature is that force which energises and enables the initiate to go onward on his quest. The main objective of the Western Quest is not withdrawal, *nirvana*, *shanti*, but a desire to serve the rest of Creation by finding and bringing back the Grail of Wisdom by whose waters the whole world will be healed, the Wasteland made green again (for it *has* been green!) To serve, it is necessary to be there, an integral part of the Creation which you are healing, helping or guiding, for the Initiate becomes the link between the Inner Earth, the place of sacred power and the people of the world who do not know about that energising and healing force which is within them.

It is the initial recognition that there is a spirit within us from which guidance, power and healing can be requested, the first step on the path to true 'self-knowledge' which is the key to the Mysteries of the West.

CHAPTER ONE

Life-Track

Each man's life is a labyrinth at the centre of which lies his death, and even after death it may be that he passes through a final maze before it is all ended for him. Within the great maze of a man's life are many smaller ones, each seemingly complete in itself, and in passing through each one, he dies in part, for in each he leaves behind a part of his life, and it lies dead behind him. It is a paradox of the labyrinth that its centre appears to be the way to freedom.

Michael Ayrton, THE MAZE MAKER

The paradox expressed in the above quotation is a true and accurate description of the life of a Seeker after Magic. It clearly depicts the entwined path of the initiate, sometimes seeming almost to reach the centre and then finding himself back near the entrance. Like the labyrinth, which is three-dimensional, whereas a maze is two-dimensional, the traveller is expected to climb up to new heights, and to sink down into tunnels and passages. He will enter great halls filled with light, and discover dark cupboards matted with cobwebs where he will encounter fearful creatures from the depths of his own being. He will find treasures which crumble to dust in the light of ordinary consciousness, and gain jewels of experience which are beyond price for they do not vanish like Faery gold.

To many a traveller the journey from the cradle to the grave is a long and dreadful experience, punctuated throughout its entire length with a series of unpleasant events over which he has no control, like the discipline and torments of school days, ill health, joblessness or some soul-destroying occupation, forced upon him by circumstances, the 'authorities', the 'state' or any other external system which he feels unable to combat or change. Between the crushing walls of 'conformity', the 'done thing' and other people's opinions lies a cruel and jagged path along which he is forced to make his way, with no options, always striving to fit into someone else's stereotype – employee, parent, husband, student, son, worker or even religious follower. Although there may be choices along the way, no one has told him he is free to make them, to turn aside, to experiment with new alternatives, in lifestyle, in religious pattern, in philosophy or relationships. These variations are hidden from him by a wall of ignorance, built of disinformation, cemented together with fear, superstition and scorn for any unconventional thoughts or acts. In order to seek out an alternative way towards freedom and self-awareness he has immediately to turn his back on this passage to orthodoxy and hack his way through the wilderness of other people's opinions or hearsay, and step forward, alone, into the unknown. He will be guided only by his personal curiosity, determination and some inner urge to explore, and eventually, to know.

It is possible to go through life driven and shaped entirely by external circumstances and the pattern of our society, but anyone who makes an act of self-determination in any field of life begins to escape the stereotype, and begins to become an individual. It doesn't matter which path someone takes, whether it be towards expertise in practical skill, excellence in sport, academic achievement or magic: each is a way towards fulfilling the prophecy of 'having Life in abundance'. The first step, which takes a Seeker out of the surging masses, who move like robots along well-defined and deep grooves, will show him a wide vista, full of exciting concepts and the promise of exploration into worlds which are totally new to him.

The magical arts are ancient, they cover a wide span of human activities; to master them requires a lot of effort on the part of the Seeker, but it is never too late to accept the alternative way, to put aside the well-trodden and conventional road and enter the wilderness. It is, however, never too soon to examine your own aims and objectives, to look at your motives and what you expect magic to do for you, and also to assess the cost to you in terms of effort and time and other resources. It is very easy for the outsider to see only the glamorous, exciting and totally *fictional* side of the occult. Books, films, and TV exposés all tend towards the dramatic and sensational aspects of these ancient and hidden technologies, focusing their words, pictures and cameras on the 'naked witches' sabbat; the fascinating 'weapons' and paraphernalia used by magicians, ancient and modern; the intriguing and brightly illustrated Tarot cards and other symbolic systems; the enchanting ideas of spells, charms, talismans, grimoires or books of magic words, which so often feature, usually out of context, in novels and plays. The sad thing is that most of these things are relevant; they do have a proper and potent place within the vast system which can be encompassed by the term 'occult'. Like the tools of a plumber there are instruments which clear blockages – not in drains but in psychic fields; there are 'talismans' which are instructions in one language to be effected in another medium, just as the notes and symbols on a sheet of music can be turned into sounds through the medium of the musical instrument, and be appreciated with senses other than the eyes. In every instance the magical equipment has exact parallels in other technologies. The Tarot symbols are like the electronic engineer's technical drawings: each symbol represents a different component which, in circuit, will act in a specific way. The magician's robe and magical circle of protection are like the laboratory overalls and sterile atmosphere found in medical research – used for exactly the same reasons, keeping the psychic rather than the physical atmosphere pure and untainted. Just as the engineer, musician, researcher, artist or any other creative worker needs training in understanding the technical jargon, the special symbols, the history and 'state of the art' of his subject, and the practical experience to put that knowledge into effect, so too does the magician. You can't become a scientist, a doctor or even a pop star overnight – you need many years of study and practical learning before anything is gained. The same applies to magic.

Just as there are electronic engineers, civil engineers and mechanical engineers, each working on a different scale, in a different field, there are ritual magicians, there are solo magicians or shamans, and there are witches and wizards, to use rather old-fashioned terms, who are members of a lodge or coven, and form an individual, yet vital, part of a team. There is an enormous range of material from the meaning of *abracadabra* to the influences of the signs of the zodiac. There is the entire history of humanity on earth, for recent research has shown that some of the earliest identifiable artefacts have carvings of the moon's phases on them, or appear to be pictures of shamans, dressed in antlered animal skins acting out a fertility or hunting ritual. Both these sources go back to the Stone Age. But magical arts have moved on, and you are just as likely to find computers and floppy discs in the magician's home today as you are ancient papyri and carved stones. Each in its own age has served a similar purpose, storing and recording information, helping to calculate the positions of the planets, encoding and passing knowledge down through the aeons. The span of required understanding is vast, it is timeless, and unless a Seeker sets out with some sort of a plan or desire, then the paths through the maze are bewildering and the journey to wisdom becomes impossible.

The first subject to study, whether you aim to become a magician or witch, a shaman or a healer, a diviner or talisman maker, is to look at who you are, where you have come from, and – perhaps most important – what prompted you to set out through the labyrinth, and what you expect to discover in the centre. You alone will appreciate what talents you already have, what skills, what interests, what mental or physical attributes which will help you on your own voyage of discovery, which will lead you from your safe and comfy armchair to the vast emptinesses in the universe where the stars no longer shine. These invisible tracks will take you to the endless caverns within the inner earth, and through the forgotten ways through your own psyche, your memory, your stores of dreams and images, desires and will, through time and space which is eternally immanent, for it is always within. It is from these unexplored sources that you will build the ability to travel through time, recalling, if you wish, who you have been, and all the knowledge you have had in previous incarnations.

You will need to look very hard at what you desire to achieve and possibly learn some hard lessons about what is need and what is greed, so that you come to know what magic will help you attain, and where only material ways will bring you to your goal. You have to begin with who you are and what place in the world and along your own life-track you inhabit now. When you learn something practical it will cause you to think in a different way, and as you read or are taught something new, it will cause you to act in the light of that new information. The two aspects cannot be dealt with separately. Gradually you will discover at least one more dimension to this knowledge, that of the Inner Way, or path of spiritual enlightenment.

A large part of all magical work will be dealt with in a realm which is not the world as most of us consider it to be. The magician will talk of the Inner Planes, the Astral World, of Masters and Contacts, and these unlikely concepts are seldom explained, except in occult dictionaries, which are never to hand when you need them. We are used to thinking only in terms of the solid reality, the 'here and now' world which we can see, and feel, hear and appreciate with all our physical senses. Yet much of what we take to be real has been learned as we grow up. Red is not a dangerous colour, yet we are taught that a red light on a traffic signal is a warning, and that it is dangerous to cross the road when it shines. We may fear spiders, which in Britain are both small and harmless, or we may be frightened of snakes, although it is unlikely we would come across any of the poisonous sort outside the safe confines of a zoo. Many people have strong fears about flying, although plane travel is demonstrably safer than crossing the road on foot! Some of these strong emotions of disquiet or even terror come from the realms within ourselves, and personal experience will demonstrate how powerful these fears can be.

A magician does not sit down and try to *prove* there is life after death, or that there are Intelligences which may not be visible during ordinary waking consciousness; he initially accepts this as a working theory, but through personal discovery soon is able, at least in his own terms, to know these concepts as true and real. Belief is taken only as a feeble scaffold set up to support the structure of personal experience until that inner structure is tall enough and strong enough to support itself. A magician does not say 'I believe,' but he says '*I KNOW!*' This applies in the fields of magical knowledge, ordinary understanding and religious experience. In every case it is experience that counts.

Magic consists, to a large extent, of seeing ordinary things in a different light. One of the greatest tools for this any magician has is that of 'imagination'. In the modern world 'imagination' is frowned upon, and phrases like 'It's all in your imagination,' are used scornfully. The first reversal of everyday interpretation you will need to understand is that 'imagination' is the single most important concept for any modern Seeker. The word 'imagine' comes from the same root as 'Magi,' denoting the biblical Wise Men, who used their 'magical' divinatory and astrological powers to trace the birthplace of the Christ Child. Another root word is, in English, 'make'. It means 'to create', to form and to craft. Where does the inspiration and power to 'make' come from? From the 'imagination', that vast power to form not only 'images' but real things. Imagination can be seen as the inner skill to make things or events come into being.

Knowledge is a skill everyone has to a certain degree. It is built up in part from memory. If you have seen a thing before, you will 'remember' what it was when you see it again. Even if you encounter something new, as an adult you will have enough data stored in your memory to be able to classify the new 'thing' as a certain kind of object. Memory may not give you the name of the new 'thing' but it will help identify it as a book, a plane, a plant or a mechanical object of no known use. When you begin to study magic you have to build up a similar store of memory encompassing all the symbols, shapes, names and related concepts which make up the enormous battery of 'magical correspondences'. A simple example might be the Moon. You could perform a Moon ritual or make a lunar talisman to improve your dream recall, for example. The Moon is a familar sight in the night or evening sky and her colour is silvery white. As she waxes and wanes she may seem bright or dim, and so her symbolic metal is silver, whose shiny surface may become tarnished and dull, but be polished to a shine again. Her day is Monday (Moon-day), and her shape is often depicted as the two-sided crescent. Her jewel is, not surprisingly, moonstone, and the goddesses of the Moon have names in every pantheon in the world, so depending on the tradition you are using you might call upon Diana, Arianrhod, Isis or Luna to bless your talisman and help it to work. The word 'Moon' is not the moon in the sky but if you see it written on paper you understand what is meant because your memory supplies a picture or other concept of 'moon'. The symbols are not 'moon' either but they act on inner aspects of our own consciousness, which are shared with all humankind, which acknowledges the idea 'moon', and through those links strengthens our individual communication with the part of our nature ruled by the Moon. Usually this helps to bring dreams into better focus so that they can be remembered and explored for meaning. Perhaps you will have to take my word for it at present, but if you make a simple

Moon talisman and place it under your pillow, and each night, before you fall asleep, during the two weeks of a waxing (growing), Moon, make a plea on the lines of 'Lady Moon, help me to remember/understand/control/or learn from my dreams, and as your silver light grows, may my dreams grow brighter too' (choosing only *one* of the options), and if you remember to do this *every night* for a fortnight, you may well be amazed at what happens.

One of the hardest things about mastering magic is that it is always difficult to know where to begin. There are dozens of books on rituals, on Qabalah, on witchcraft, astrology, tantra, Zen – even the words may not make any sense to you as yet! Again the question has to be considered by each Seeker for himself. Do you wish to share the drama and theatricals of participating in ceremonial lodge magic, or would you prefer simpler solo talisman making? Do you long for the wild woods and the call of the Goddess in the midnight air? Do you wish to become a healer, or a reader of Tarot cards or rune stones? Do you want to benefit only yourself, aiming to gain power over people, as some books promise, the ability to command others at a distance, and always have them obey your will? (How would you like to be on the receiving end of such a magical power, being made to bow to the wishes of another person, obey his will, be forced to work or love or act to the command of any other? Well, think very hard before you launch yourself into a career of selfishness and greed.) There are very strong ethical forces at work in the Inner Worlds, where the seeds of magic grow into reality. They tend to act in triplicate, and are often referred to as the 'Law of Threefold Return'. This means that if you do anything which the Inner considers harmful, *you* will receive three times that amount of ill luck. Equally, if you do good, then you gain in terms of good luck. It may not happen all at once, but over the years the balance will be remade. You will also find that whatever power you had will have vanished, and the paths of the endless labyrinth will close in around you. This is not intended as a veiled threat, but having seen the working out of *karma*, the universal law of action and reaction, in magic, I know that this law cannot be avoided if you set off, deliberately to flaunt the rules of decent human behaviour. Certainly the Lords of Karma, the Inner Guardians whom you are certain to encounter on your wanderings, are fair. They will not harm the blundering novice who makes mistakes, but they are ever-watchful, and absolutely *real*.

The Way to the Centre is not of itself dangerous; nor is ordinary living, but there are dangers, such as thoughtlessness: even in the material world, a moment's inattention can end with you under a bus. You can encounter things which frighten you, because you do not know what they are. In the Inner worlds, at least to begin with, you will be on unfamiliar territory, and you will have no experience to judge the validity or power or intention of anything you encounter there. Driven on, between the climbing shelves of unread information on the one hand, and the desire to know, to experience and to dare on the other, you will edge further into this maze, bringing with you only that which *is* you. What you fear on the Inner Path will be a reflection of what you fear outside, and although it may be only a reflection, and not the frightful thing itself, it will affect you none the less. Gradually, you will learn to recognise those characters, symbols and experiences which are helpful, and shun those which do not help, but this takes time.

You will always be forced back to re-examine your own objectives, your own skills, your desires and aims. You will need to explore your own qualities in the four fields of life, in magic determined by the Four Elements, of earth, water, fire and air. Each will provide you with strengths and each with handicaps. Earth is the foundation of your character, your physical make-up, the skills of persistence and practicality, and from its roots the more delicate parts of your True Self have grown. Like the planet Earth it gives you a home and foundation, but it is rigid, strong and immovable, and you are a being who needs freedom to move and change, not a tree in a forest, forever rooted to the spot, to be swayed by wind, and shaped by weather. The water part of you will also need to be understood, for this is the part of you which feels and senses. It is what links you to other people, just as the river or sea divides and yet joins the shores on either side. To some people this is an insurmountable barrier, to others it is a convenient medium for travel. You cannot work magic without feeling, for the greatest power comes from love and trust, desire and pleasure, as you will eventually discover. The trouble with water is that its liquid state causes it to flow and meander, and only by knowing where and when it is useful, and controlling it by some other element in your being, will you make it serve you faithfully.

Fire gives you energy, drive, determination and courage, lots of which will be required from you in the pursuit of magical power.

It is also the uncontrolled feelings of hot-blooded anger, of untamed fear, of fright and flight when you cannot hold that force in check. Air is the element of mind and thoughts, memory, wishes and intuition. It is least tangible, and although modern science has not been able to separate mind and brain, the magician has to be able to divide wisdom from curiosity, knowledge from guesswork, fact from symbolic fiction in many aspects of his work.

Understanding these factors in your own life, past and present, is one of the earliest tasks to be faced on your journey through the maze. Take time, and quietly examine your own progress, dividing it up under the Four Elements. Only you can fairly judge your physical, emotional, mental and intellectual state, apportioning your known and familiar feelings into these categories. Everyone's Life-Track is a long and convoluted one, even if your span of years is not all that great, for much of it may have been lived beyond recall, in previous lives and places. Only by patiently trying to understand where you are now and then deciding where you would like to go next can you hope to make a wise choice as to the immediate next step – just as when looking at a map for directions you have to know where you *are* before you can decide which way to go.

Another of the paradoxes of magic can best be expressed by the idea of 'hastening slowly'. Many of the most elaborate and complicated rituals or metaphysical activities go on in another level of reality, inside the head, or rather within the limitless confines of the magician's imagination. The more experienced you get, the clearer it will become that stillness and silence, confidence and knowledge, a clear aim and patience are the things which actually make magic work. The arts of divination require the diviner to become absolutely still and focused totally on the cards or other symbols, so that he can read the writing on both sides of the labyrinth. On the one hand there is the typical meaning of each card, learned from a book or teacher, and on the other is the inner intuitive guidance. In all good readings these two factors are balanced and combined. You cannot be accurate just by going 'by the book', and you can't always make inspired guesses when using an unfamiliar divination system.

The hardest things for new Seekers to learn are those arts requiring repeated practice, complete physical stillness and silent, inward-turned thinking. These are hard to learn and there is no substitute for doing them, again and again, until they become second nature. Often these basic meditative arts are not learned as quickly as they might be because the student doesn't understand what 'remain absolutely still and relax' means! Most people have become used to being restless, shifting position, not concentrating fully on what is going on inside their heads, because no one has ever pointed out how valuable these basic arts are. Sitting quietly, with your eyes closed on a hard, upright chair seems a long way from the drama described in any occult novel in which powerful magicians and priestesses, in full regalia, carry out complex rituals in elaborate ancient temples, filled with the swirling smoke of exotic incenses. Like much of occult fiction, this is based on fact – the above could be High Mass at any Roman Catholic cathedral in the world. It could be the coronation of a monarch, or consecration of a bishop. It could, toned down to a mere handful of highly skilled and experienced magicians, be a working for world peace, wisdom or brotherhood. However, the vast majority of real magical work is done by dedicated people who have spent many years learning to sit very still and withdraw their controlled consciousness, and then refocus it where it is needed. They can experience the colours and sounds of robes, smell the incense, hear the chanting, and help build up the patterns of power used to bring their will into being, but these are not visible to the outsider.

If you want to begin or continue your own path through the magical labyrinth you will need to begin with some extremely simple yet absolutely vital exercises. You will need to spend at least fifteen minutes every single day sitting quiet and still and musing over aspects of your own personality, life and ambitions. If you have an astrological chart, you will have a starting-point. You do not need to know very much astrology to begin with so long as you know which of the signs are ruled by which of the Four Elements

Earth – Taurus, Virgo, Capricorn.
Water – Cancer, Scorpio, Pisces
Fire – Aries, Leo, Sagittarius
Air – Gemini, Libra, Aquarius.

Each of the planets of a chart will lie in one of the above signs, and so it will take on a little of the nature of the element. See how many you have in each element, are you all Airey-Fairy, Down-to-Earthy, Wishy-washy-Watery, or Irey-Firey, always springing into action without a thought. Are you *actually* like that?

You need to look at what you have achieved in the world, in very ordinary terms. How did you get on at school? Have you had any further education, or would you like to learn more later in life? (People still get university degrees at the age of 70 + !) Do you prefer *doing* to *thinking*, or *dreaming* to *acting*? These too relate to your elemental balance.

How do you get on with the people around you? Are you a loner or a family person? Have you dozens of friends or only a few? Do you have lots of acquaintances but no *real* friends? Magic is often a co-operative activity and you will need to be able to get on with other people. In the more advanced stages your whole success and magical survival can depend on your ability to rely on others and work as a part of a team. What about your relationships with sexual partners? How do you see them, as real people or as stereotypes fitting some dreamed-up image? Do they love you honestly, and do you give out love? Do you know the difference between being *in love* and *loving*? What about lust? Are you happy when outnumbered at a gathering of members of the opposite sex? Are you happier when only in the company of your own sex? Do you find working with groups or individuals in a close society easy or difficult? How do you cope when you are forced into the company of someone you actively dislike? How do people who don't like you react to your presence? It is as well to look at some of these social interactions, for it is certain that if you ever enter any kind of magical group or coven you will come up against the personalities of those around you – and magicians, as a bunch, tend to have very strong characters! You certainly won't be able to start off as a leader, but will have to learn from others, rub shoulders, in very close and quite strange circumstances with people you don't necessarily know well.

It is no good hanging a label like 'Pagan' or 'Witch' or 'Magician' around your neck and expecting everyone to like you immediately because you have selected a cosy stereotype to hide behind. The same applies to being black, gay, left-handed, Jewish or any other sort of minority. Being one of a self-defined sort says nothing about you! How friendships and magical relationships work is on a much more individual level. People are all absolutely different, individual and unique, and by studying magic they should always strive to enhance this uniqueness, not by setting up as the 'Great and Only One' but by using their own personality to build upon. If you are competent, capable, friendly, lovable and honest, these qualities will be recognised and you will be valued for them. Why exclude yourself from contact with people who would automatically shun the label you are so keen to wear? You will do a lot more to counteract prejudice by being a respected and well-liked individual who also admits to wanting to be part of some minority. Grow into the greatest being you are capable of becoming; certainly you will find that magical skills enhance not only the outward aspects of your individuality, but those subtle inner facets of personality which are reflections of your immortal soul.

Another aspect of your self you will need to look at with magical eyes is your Inner Self. Carl Jung writes about the anima in men and the animus in women, showing that the 'soul' is of the opposite sex to that of the physical body. This fact has been long acknowledged in magical philosophy, and on this basis an individual's relationship with the gods and goddesses can be built. When you are dealing in the magical sense with gods and goddesses you are not merely a worshipper, acting through a priest, but you become a priest or priestess in your own right. Gradually you make a link with the Inner Self and through that contact the goddess or god who is always, at one level, within you. Once you accept that you are holy, that part of you is eternal, and that an essential, inner aspect of you reflects the opposite sex, it will help you understand all kinds of relationships and facets of your personality. When the link has been truly forged you will find that, in Aleister Crowley's definition, you will have Knowledge and Conversation with your Holy Guardian Angel. You will *know* the gods and goddesses, for they are within. Like the Moon you are able to shine by the reflected light of their solar star being. You too will begin to cast forth a light which can lead others along the path, instead of casting a shadow from the dim candle of someone else's priesthood. Acknowledge those spiritual things within you which are good, which need strengthening and which can become the greatest power for good on earth. Seek out that same spark in all the people around you. Sense it in your beloved, your children and in the total strangers you encounter every day. As your magical awareness of Self grows, so will your perception of the nature of other people be reflected in that mirror of consciousness within you. Do not overlook the fact that you are a precious, unique individual in the eyes of the Eternal, living in a world of other individual jewels.

Allow that inner spark to shine through by polishing it with self-knowledge and personal honesty, and with acceptance and love of the person you happen to be in this incarnation.

If you are willing to see clearly who you are now, grown from who you were as a child, and what you will progress to become, if you so will it, you can unravel the pattern of your individual being. Later on you may well come to recognise that you have lived other lives in other bodies and other lands. Through the gates of meditation you can re-enter the previous string of incarnations, once you have gained the key by dedicated effort. When you can see that you have had other lives and also other deaths, you will be able to face that last taboo of the civilised world – the fear of death.

In magic, death is a very important concept to come to terms with. In the oldest temples of teaching, when the initiate was accepted into the order of the wise he would go through a symbolic death. Not in the modern dramatic way of lying down and then arising ten minutes later as a member of a coven or lodge, but by actually entering a tomb in a cave or tumulus, and by sinking down through the levels of consciousness to a near-death state in which he would remain until he had experienced his soul passing through the gates of death into the great beyond, and then returning to the light, reborn. That is why initiates are often referred to as the 'Twice-Born'; they have died while still living, and being dead they have been reborn as children of the gods. If you follow the maze path to the centre, that might be your own experience. To the magician, death is only a new starting-point, a renewal and not the end.

CHAPTER TWO

By-Ways of the Mind

The Nine Men's Morris is fill'd up with mud,
And the Quaint mazes on the wanton green,
For lack of tread are indistinguishable.

Titania in MIDSUMMER NIGHT'S DREAM

To most people there are two obvious states of awareness: being awake, and being asleep or unconscious for some reason. To the Seeker there are many more options than that because he knows that magic involves changes in his consciousness, which he controls and directs. You may well have read about meditation and creative visualisation, image-building or pathworking as it is sometimes called, as well as things like astral travel, out of the body experiences, directed dreams and prophetic visions, without knowing exactly what each is and how it might be experienced. All of these involve states of mind other than those of ordinary waking consciousness or of sleep. We will look at some of them below.

You will have to begin by accepting that there are many interconnected levels of consciousness, most of which are natural and usually occur on the threshold of sleep, in untrained people.

This is called by psychologists a 'hypnogogic' state and can be recognised as the pleasant, relaxed but very brief moment which happens as you fall asleep each night, and recurs just as you wake up. Over the thousands of years which magical ideas have taken to develop, lots of effort has been given to learning to control this hypnogogic state. It requires the individual to be able consciously to relax his body, in magic, by taking up an upright, well-supported yet comfortable position and allowing the attention to be redirected to another level, beyond that of ordinary awareness. Entry into this state, with practice, takes only seconds, and during it you can be as aware or unaware of sounds and events around you as you wish, and you may remain still and relaxed for as long as you need; between ten and forty-five minutes is common. At the end you come fully and quickly back to ordinary waking consciousness being able to remember all the ideas and concepts which have flowed through your mind. By starting off with a particular symbol, phrase, image, story or god-form, for example, you will gradually find 'new' ideas enter your head and become knowledge. From nowhere meditation seems to bring forth pieces of data or clarify things you thought you knew. This process is called 'Realisation', that is, it makes real the object of your meditation and expands your knowledge of it without you reading a book or being told about it.

Meditation takes a lot of practice which should be regular and continuous for many weeks or perhaps months before a steady flow of new, or at least relevant, material starts to trickle past your point of inner awareness, to the exclusion of all those annoying and distracting thoughts which so plague the newcomer to the art. Recent research has shown that actual changes in the chemistry of the blood occur during and after a session of meditation, just as similar chemical changes occur during and after a period of sport or jogging. During meditation the body becomes relaxed and the stress chemicals in the blood are gradually reduced, so that afterwards you not only feel calmer but continue to do so for some time. As this is a slow process it improves with regular and consistent meditations, but the advantages are twofold: on one hand you will feel mentally calmer and less anxious, and secondly, the realisations which come from each meditation will come more readily and distinctly. After a lot of practice it is only a matter of a minute or two to re-enter the place of inner stillness and revelation, receive guidance or new knowledge and bring it back into the light of full and peaceful awareness.

To learn to meditate requires quite a few changes from your ordinary waking state. You will need a comfortable, but supportive, upright chair. You will need relative peace and quiet, and a time and place set aside from mundane worries. You will need a notebook and pen to jot down your realisations (or the lack of them to begin with). You will also require perseverance in making regular attempts, even if nothing seems to be happening, especially at the beginning, when all the physical and mental distractions will be at their worst.

The inner levels of the consciousness are not usually exposed to the light of understanding except, obscurely, during dreams, or those mindless moments of mental drift which used to be called 'day-dreaming'. There are strong doors which separate these levels of mind and memory and greater awareness which seems to come from somewhere beyond every individual's personal store of knowledge. This has a double function. Its main one is to prevent the continual overlap of experience. For example, if you taste an orange, you recognise the flavour and texture but you don't remember every other orange you have ever eaten, or smelt, or seen, because you would be totally overwhelmed. The doors also close your consciousness off from that of other people, keeping it safely locked into a narrow slot of time called 'now', in a place called 'here'. The magician is taught that consciousness can be trained to reach out beyond those imposed confines, but he has to maintain a rigid control so that his impressions stay within his own limits, and can be coped with as is necessary. Unless this control is always there, your awareness is completely flooded by memories of past and future, the feelings and thoughts of other people around you, and the massive amount of sensed data which is bombarding you the whole time. You would see, hear, feel, taste and smell vast amounts of things, and each of those would evoke within your mind all the previous associations. You would be drowned out by these floods of sensations and very quickly go mad. As you learn the arts of mind-control, be it the passive and receptive art of meditation, or the more active, creative art of visualisation, you gain control over the doors for yourself, so that they can be opened a crack at will, and then shut very firmly until you have had a chance to assimilate the information received.

Many of the arts of divination also rely on this control of the sluice-gates of consciousness, for by gently probing the mind of the questioner, and relating that knowledge to the symbols of the Tarot cards, a competent diviner can extract a helpful and relevant answer to a query. The only way such control can be gained is by allowing yourself to explore gradually the untrodden and overgrown maze that is your own inner mind. You will often come up against blank walls, or be forced to return again and again to the same path until the unseen doors can be found and opened, and closed at will, with the key you will find through persisting with the training exercises. The mind-maze is vast. It is on many levels and many time-tracks, as you will soon discover. You may have to force yourself to meditate for ten minutes to begin with, but soon you will gain certainty that what you are doing is right. You will know by getting new information and those bridging concepts which link up a variety of pieces of knowledge into a clearer picture, which make you say 'Aha!' to yourself, and time will cease to have any meaning. A good meditation need only take twenty minutes but you can feel as if you had been exploring for hours, just as your time-sense in dreams is relative.

Learning to travel beyond time is an important factor in journeying in the realms of inner consciousness, for it will ultimately allow you to discover all sorts of things about your own past, right through this life, and if you have the courage and the key, those earlier, other lives, too. By gradually revisiting all the events of your current life and seeing them from a new viewpoint, dispassionately, it is possible to learn many valuable lessons that the pain of failure, the fear of the unknown, self-doubt and other inbuilt inhibitors prevented you from learning at the time the original events took place. Now you have a new dimension through which you can explore these feelings, fears, hopes and achievements, for meditation will show you the way.

Meditation will cause permanent changes in the way you think and in the way you see the world around you. Often these changes are not as pleasant as you might imagine. Your waking awareness is forced to give up the phoney shields behind which it has protected itself from the outside world. Mind journeys are not an escape from reality, but a deeper and often more painful entry into it. You will be faced with the true vision of what other people think and feel about you, and the only way to come to terms with it is to accept, and then rethink your attitude to your relationships with them. Many people imagine that to dive into the peace and calm of the inner realms will immediately and permanently rid them of everyday hassles with their nearest and dearest ones. This just isn't so. Within the mind-fields you will have to face all the aspects of your own being, and your soul will be bared in a landscape which has nothing tangible to hide behind. You will have your eyes opened and may well not like what you see there.

Some people feel that they will be harmed by this voyage of inner exploration, that they will fall prey to some lurking dark force, and become scared before taking even the first simple step towards ultimate enlightenment. Certainly there is a Guardian at the Gate, there are dark and strange beings there, but they are all part of you, the Seeker. The Guardian is there for your protection, he is a friend in armour so you cannot see his face, but you must approach him, tell him your true desire, ask his help on the long and winding path through the hidden city within, which is his own territory. He is the keeper of the Doors of Consciousness and it is by his bidding that you will gain the key of control of those doors. He is the protector of those shadowed areas of thought and pain which do not need to be shown forth immediately, but looked at gradually as your confidence and awareness increase.

It is the Guardian who sets the small tests for any new meditator, who causes the nose to itch, or the knee to tickle, just as you sit down and start to relax. It is he who feeds out those random thoughts about mundane troubles and cares which are so distracting and cannot be quelled by telling them to go away. The only way to overcome these niggles is to concentrate on the purpose of the meditation. See clearly the symbol, or hear the phrase spoken, or the imagery revealed. Examine it behind your shut eyelids in greater and greater detail. You cannot 'make your mind go blank', but you can deliberately refocus your attention on what is at that moment important, and that is the way to defeat the Guardian's trap. It requires effort, concentration as well as physical relaxation. It is another of the paradoxes of magic.

Many of the magical mind-states require what can most simply be expressed as 'dual consciousness'. In this state it is possible, for example, to be following the theme of a meditation through the scenes or symbols which pass by the mind's eye, and also observe the actual process too. This kind of dual awareness is particularly necessary when you come to perform elaborate rituals because then it is necessary to be essentially in 'two places at once'. Part of you must remain fully aware of your physical location, be it in or out of doors, and the other part of your awareness can 'see' and 'sense' the location of the ritual, for example an Egyptian Temple, or Stonehenge, or whatever scenario the particular ritual demands.

Recent research has shown that the two hemispheres of which the largest parts of our brains are made up, have distinct and different functions. The left-hand side, which, on the whole, controls the right-hand side of our bodies, deals with language, logical and linear thinking, the sorts of subjects which are learned at school, and often thought of as 'masculine' thinking modes. The right side of the brain controls the left side of the body, and its methods of cognition are much more intuitive, spacial, connective and visual rather than literary. In some ways this could be thought of as 'feminine' cognition. Magic requires the balance of both!

Yet another complication with which the magician comes to terms is the fact that his inner spirit is female, and that of a woman is male. Dr Carl Jung gave these aspects of the inner self the titles of anima in men and animus in women. Recognising the validity of the concept is important because when you come to deal with the gods and goddesses of the magical worlds, you will need to use the inner and outer spiritual links to get to know them. This 'opposite sex within' idea may often be encountered during some meditations, because in these a Guide or Companion may appear to your mind's eye, to lead you, guard you or explain things to you, as you proceed through the labyrinth. This Guide is yet another part of your own psyche, and, if treated as a friend, will lead you safely. If you are rude or thoughtless or demanding, you will be tricked and confused, for the Guide's reality is different from yours, and he or she can get you very lost in the hidden lands. Learn to accept your anima or animus as a reliable leader, familiar with those regions of your inner self which your outer consciousness cannot usually approach, and you will travel safely, at will, and learn a great deal from that endless source of wisdom.

Through regular sessions of meditation you will begin to recognise the stages of physical relaxation. You will find that your breathing and heartbeat slow and become steady. There are a variety of ways of bringing these changes about, under your own control. The Eastern way is often to use the chanting of a *mantra*, a word or pattern of sounds repeated out loud or in the head until it becomes meaningless, leading you through the doors of altered awareness. To the Western mind this can be distracting and unless it is used properly, for a long enough time, nothing obvious happens. Chanting will often have an effect on consciousness for purely physical reasons, as it alters the amount of oxygen in your blood and brain. This can be harmful, for it may deprive the brain of its vital supply of life-giving oxygen and lead to a faint, or it can lead to hyperoxygenation, and again be the cause of dizziness and nausea.

Another Eastern method often used is 'counting the breath'. In this exercise you concentrate on each breath you take, counting a specific number for each inhalation, while you hold your breath, as you breathe out, and again with the breath held out. As a way of distracting the mind while the body relaxes, it can work, but often you get so wound up in counting, which is a left-brain function, that the intuitive and creative right side of the brain can't get a thought in edgeways, and it is that source of inspiration and intuition which Western meditation is aimed at awakening. Sometimes you can usefully try counting the breath as a way of relaxation, but the Western way is to feel the pulse in your wrist or, if you concentrate, in your neck without having to touch it, and breathing in, holding the breath in, breathing out, and holding it out, each for a certain number of regular pulse beats. Gradually the rhythm is established and you can breathe very regularly, gradually getting slower as you relax into a new state. Try each, and discover which of the various patterns is most helpful. You can count the same number for each of the four stages, or have a very long slow in and out with a short hold, and so on. Some of these patterns may make you feel calm and still, others are exhilarating and energising.

What you will find, if you meditate regularly, over a matter of weeks, is that if you count your pulse for a minute before each session, and then again at the end of the twenty minutes or so, there should be a definite slowing down, which may increase as you get the hang of the art. If you have access to any biofeedback equipment you will also be able to see that your skin resistance will drop as you relax, usually indicated by a change of tone to a lower note on the equipment, or a lower reading on the dial. Again, over a period of time, these levels drop more and quickly, and will tend to stay lower, as you come to terms with your anxieties by getting used to the changed states and what happens in them. Meditation is a good antidote to fear, anxiety and pain, but for it to be effective when you need it, you will have to become proficient by regular practice first.

Meditation is the first art to master on the path through the maze, for it is the one which controls the doors to inner awareness. It is a passive, negative and receptive state, where, once you have allowed the change of focus to take place, you wait for ideas, pictures, senses, concepts and new information to flow along the observed train of thought which the method brings to light. It will happen quite quickly, once you get the knack, but that won't usually happen until you have been at it for weeks, or months (or occasionally years!). You do need to be patient. Everyone can meditate if they can be bothered to make the continuing effort. Children can be taught to as soon as they are able to understand about relaxing and being still. Old age pensioners can learn meditation and benefit from it as an excellent cheap, safe and effective way of overcoming pain and stiffness, in both body and mind!

Sit still and upright, so that your back is straight, supported on cushions if necessary. Being physically still is a real part of the art, for a small movement of one person in a group can disturb all, and no one gets results. Become inwardly still and be aware of breathing slowly, deeply and naturally. Tell yourself to continue doing so throughout the whole session. Allow the symbol, phrase or what have you which is the theme of the meditation to flow gently into awareness. Allow it to lead you through images, feelings, sensations, sounds, scents or any other aspects of your own awareness. Let part of you flow with the trend, and allow a part to carry on a kind of running commentary, so that you remember each stage of the inner journey, or each symbol as it occurs. This helps you to remember the scenes when you have completed the meditation, and it is vital that you write, draw or record on tape as much (or at the beginning, as little) of what you have perceived so that you can build up new knowledge. Meditation is quite a complex art, although in essence it is simple. You will come to grips with this paradox only by doing it regularly for a few months, and being able to look back at your notes and see how far you have progressed.

The twin activity with meditation, which should follow it as soon as you get regular results, is that of creative visualisation. Whereas meditation is receptive and passive, creative visualisation uses the same state of altered consciousness but does so in a positive way. In meditation, you watch and listen, feel and absorb, in creative visualisation you build, imagine and explore in a very active way. Although doing this with visual images, pictures, symbols, shapes, colours and things which you can see with your mind's eye, many people, particularly men who work with words, computers or logic, find it very hard to *see* anything. I am sure they actually *can* see these inner landscapes, but don't recognise them except as 'imagination', pretending they are not real, because in their world view, only the physical world is real! It does take a quantum jump to be able to accept that there are other forms of reality, each equally valid, and many people don't wish to sacrifice their long-held beliefs. Again, once you are able to experience the inner worlds they become real and you don't need to argue with yourself as to whether they are real or not.

You may find you feel atmospheres, sense objects, smell scents which are alien to the physical environment, or detect vague shapes and colours; these are all ways in which the inner worlds can make themselves known if you are willing to undergo the change of consciousness necessary to take you from your world to theirs. It is a small step, but an impossible one for those who will not relinquish their firm hold on one sort of reality, and step through the filmy veil which blinds their sight from the endless options within. Practice, dedication, continued effort and a willingness to allow changes in state to occur are vital to the mastery of the art of creative visualisation, without which no true magic can ever be performed.

Certainly the easiest way to permit this shift of level is under the personal guidance of a trained and competent magical teacher, but these have always been very thin on the ground, hard to find, and on the whole, far too busy to bother with a novice Seeker who wants to take a short-cut to astral vision, instead of wandering about the inner labyrinth on his own until he understands the pattern for himself. Sharing the learning process with other beginners is another valid and often effective approach, for then at least you can compare notes. There is no single correct way to perform any of these exercises because the Door Keeper to an individual's consciousness is personal to him. He has to find the key, the password or gesture which will gain entry, and you can't get a handy adept to come along and break down the door for you. Or if you do, you then have no way of closing the door to keep out those thoughts and impulsions, the telepathy and sensitivity which will always flow through. That is one of the genuine dangers of magical training, for it is often that a so-called 'Mage' will perform this brutal act of 'mind rape' to let the novice see for himself, without any form of control or limitation. It is a frightening experience which can lead to madness and nervous breakdown. It is perfectly possible that many people in mental institutions have somehow had these inner doors forced by some experience, the use of drugs, or even allergies to ordinary foods, chemicals or alcohol, so that they have no control. They may hear voices, as do many people, sane and mad, derived from the animus or anima, the 'conscience', and inner aspects of the mind which the magician learns to recognise and befriend.

Take great care who you deal with in these matters. If you have any doubts, hang back. Another and safer chance will come, and to find your self-awareness led astray inside the mind-maze is no fun prospect. You won't be under attack from 'black magicians' or evils lurking in the dark, but just from those unopened cupboards, those gloomy and unexplored areas of memory, of experiences repressed due to pain, or unresolved inner conflicts which an ordinary life piles up. This is the litter of a life of living, and in its own way is no more of a nuisance than the junk in the attic of your house; but mind-refuse has nowhere to go, unless it is sorted out from time to time and those aspects of it which have a purpose and use recycled into waking awareness. There will be a residue which will have to be scrapped, accepted as rubbish and cast out by a definitive act of cleansing, which is another art you will need to master when you begin to work rituals. Before you start a rite you have to clear the space to perform it in. This cleansing of the special place for even simple meditations can be another way of calming both you and the atmosphere, and of directing your attention to the subject of the meditation or visualisation exercise. (See the next chapter for details of what to do.)

When you have got somewhere with meditation you can have a go at the other side of the coin of mental training, and instead of choosing a theme and allowing the ideas to develop around it, or flow in a wide circle and return to it, as thoughts do in effective meditations, you mentally set the scene. You actually create, on another level of being, the world, the temple, the cave, the Guide or the gods which you wish to deal with. Of course, you don't actually manufacture them from your imagination, but by decid-

ing what scene you wish to witness, you learn to become aware of
that scene and no other. As you build the image inside your head,
with your eyes closed, you will discover that you can see more
and more clearly the place of your intended vision journey. (The
same concept applies if, at first, you don't actually 'see', but
appreciate with some other senses what you wish). The floor, the
walls, the people, the scents, the ambience, all gradually appear,
like a photograph slowly developing itself before your inner
sight. Again, it may take months of effort before those scenes are
real and solid, and as clear as the room around you when you
open your eyes. Eventually, the inner scene can become more real
and the 'real' world fade to a shadow for the time of the working.
Often you will be aware of both worlds superimposed upon each
other for you will find that you can open your eyes and see both
at once, although that may take a long time if your inner sight has
not been stimulated since you learned to read words on paper.

Developing the imagination is a vital part of magical training.
You need to be able to conjure up any sort of place in time or
space, to see it as real, and to be able to interact with whatever
you discover there. You will need to be able to recall the faces of
those dear to you to ask healing or help for them if they ask you.
You will need to recognise the landscapes of dreams and day-
dreams so that you know where they fit in this vast mind-scape.
You will have to start with simple exercises of recognition,
shutting your eyes and building up a picture of your own hand,
held out before you, so that you can open your eyes and compare
vision and fact, until both are the same, and the inner vision is
clear and reliable.

Do learn to observe in the world too. Know the names of trees
and their habitat, the layout of castles and stately homes, the plan
and atmosphere of great gardens, wild moors, deserted sea-
scapes, high peaks and lowland plains. Each of these has an inner
reality too. Many of them are important scenes of inner activity
which you will need to recognise at a glance when true vision is
granted to you and you become a seer. Learn about the setting of
the tradition you choose to follow. The Celtic Forest, the Egyptian Desert, the Himalayan Heights or the Atlantean Deeps – each
has its symbolic scenery, its ambience, its smells and feelings, and
each is very different.

When you begin to use creative visualisation it will be as if you
are taking items out of a vast stage set and arranging them to suit
your need. You may well begin on a small scale with a room or

temple. In it you will have to see the floor and walls, the ceiling and pillars, any altars, statues, furniture and companions. You will need to build these images, or perhaps more correctly, summon them to appear before you, as they really are in their own dimension. Look at the colours, the shapes, the sizes of things. Notice their solidity (or, at the beginning, their lack of it). Imagine something, close your inner eyes and then reopen them and see what has appeared before you. Does it look exactly as you imagined it? In other words, has your vision made it, or is it subtly different, so that what you perceive is real in the inner realms, and therefore seen as such?

The most common use of creative visualisation is in the art of pathworking, an elaborate system based on the Qabalist's Paths which join the spheres on the Tree of Life (see Glossary). As each sphere has its colour, image and symbolism, so do the paths which link them. By starting at any sphere, usually in the case of novices, at Malkuth, the Kingdom at the foot of the Tree, you progress away from the obvious imagery of the Earth as our home planet, towards, for example, the Moon, in the sphere Yesod. Don't worry if these terms mean nothing to you as yet. You are travelling on the Mind Road between the Earth and the Moon, leaving the light of day for the violet light of night. On this journey you fly through space, feeling the loss of Earth's gravity and sensing the freedom of life among the stars. When you arrive on the Moon the light is purple and the land silver, and because it is the sphere of dreams and imagination, what you see may seem unlikely. During your stay in the indigo and violet world you ought to be able to perceive new things and gain insights about the nature of the Moon and its relationship with Earth. You might see the machinery which drives and controls the universe turning about you.

Pathworking journeys can take you from your home to any-where, in time or in space. You will need to follow a route, step by step, along a country lane, through a garden, among city build-ings, into ancient sacred places, and under the earth itself, to the Otherworld, which is also the Country of the Mind. You may sit down to write these out so that you can read them on tape and listen, with your eyes closed, to the various stages of the journey. You may be in a position to share these travels with companions who can take it in turn to 'discover' and narrate these voyages of inner exploration, or you can purchase ready-recorded cassette tapes of special journeys, prepared to guide the listener to a particular place or scenario.

When you hear someone actually leading a pathworking you might begin to discover that you leap ahead of the place they are describing, seeing the next phase perfectly before they have got round to describing it. This all helps to demonstrate that the inner worlds *are* real, and that the narrator is travelling through them with you, describing each scene as he or she sees it. It takes a few moments to perceive a part of the landscape and then describe it in suitable words, so you might have moved on ahead of the description. This is a good sign, showing that you have genuinely entered that state of altered awareness in which the other world is real, and are seeing it clearly. This does take practice.

To recap on some of the ideas in this chapter, which are absolutely vital to the practice of effective and safe magic, here are a couple of basic exercises to try. Even if you are more experienced they are worth trying, just to see what happens. The first concerns meditation. Find a good upright chair which is comfortable and supports your spine well. Choose a quiet time in your house and ensure you won't be disturbed for about half an hour. Get a notebook and pen. Sit down and for a few moments concentrate on your breathing and general comfort. Allow yourself to relax, perhaps starting at the top of your head and tightening and relaxing each group of muscles, a few at a time. Screw up your face and jaw, hunch your shoulders and arms, clench your fists, tighten your chest, pull in your stomach and bottom, press your thighs together, tense your calf muscles and curl up your toes, doing each set at a time and fully relaxing it afterwards. Feel through each part of you to ensure total relaxation has occurred, going back over any bits that are still tense. Balance your head upright on your neck and close your eyes, allow waves of calmness to pour down over you, washing away tensions and distracting ideas. Become very still and quiet.

Now focus on the idea of 'Sun'. See it, feel the warmth, imagine its effect on the Earth. Allow ideas, pictures, concepts and notions to arise and with part of your awareness note these down. Let each train of thought lead on a bit but keep 'Sun' in the back of your mind so that you don't get lost. Gradually follow those concepts back to the place or thought you began with, then open your eyes, stretch, and immediately write down or draw each stage of what you perceived. Work at it, and record anything else

which pops into your mind on the subject later on. This isn't easy,
but if you persist you will succeed. Then go on to the Moon and
see what you get, and then try both together. Then look at the
Earth, and make a triangle.

While you are doing these exercises, try to notice what you are
feeling, hearing, seeing and being aware of, with not only your
refocused inner eyes, but your ordinary senses too. Many people
feel that sounds in the street, or house, the coldness of the room,
the strangeness of the experience will put them off. These are
excuses. Keep on redirecting your awareness to Sun, or Moon or
the Earth and distractions will not bother you. Stay relaxed, calm
and breathe easily, and very soon some quite strange things will
start to happen, both inside your head, and around you, in your
perception of the world. Speak gently with your inner Guardian
and he/she will help you, rather than playing tricks or teasing
you. Treat the matter as a game, as fun and you will succeed; try
too hard you and will fail, by slamming the door you seek to
open.

It is quite important that you are aware of what is happening to
you on several levels as you start to meditate, or perform any
magical arts for the first time, because it will give you confidence
that you can cope with the changes these bring. Try to see what is
happening within your mind as you gain insights on the meditation subject. Examine the stages by which you become aware of
the Vision you are creating/perceiving during the exercises. See
how thoughts and trains of ideas develop and grow, even during
the ordinary processes of problem-solving during your waking
hours. Notice the natural stages you go through when you fall
asleep, when you dream, and when you awake. Try to observe
and compare those feelings and perceptions with what happens
when you meditate. Your mental changes are likely to be peculiar
to you, so there can't be a set of hard and fast rules or steps which
you can follow for total success without fail. Meditation and
mental magics aren't like cake mixes, promising excellent results
every time. It is much more a matter of trial and error, the errors
teaching more than the successes, on the whole.

A simple experiment in creative visualisation requires that you
go through the same stages of relaxation and physical and mental
stilling as for meditation, but then imagine the following:

You are walking along a fairly familiar street. You will suddenly
notice that a building you have often seen before but have ignored

now has a shiny brass plate on the doorpost saying *MUSEUM* in big letters. The door is open and so you enter. You will see that it at first appears both dark and deserted, but as you peer into the dim interior you see a flight of curving stairs before you, and an arrow on the wall pointing upwards. You climb the wide stairs which are lit by a stained-glass window, noticing what it depicts as you pass the landing. Then there are heavy wooden doors with engraved glass in them and you push hard to open them. As they part, a strange and musty smell greets you, and in the twilight of the large room beyond you make out the shapes of glass cases, of statues, of brightly coloured items hung on the high walls, even pictures on the ceiling. It is very quiet, and no one is about. You creep carefully among the old-fashioned show cases, some of which are covered with faded velvet cloths, which you may gently lift to peer underneath. What you see will in many ways be limited by what you need to know. This is a museum not a shop, so you can only bring away memories. The museum is not yet fully open; its displays are not labelled and some of their purposes may well be obscure. There are other items in packing cases, not yet revealed, and some things might be taken away to other museums. You will have to look about you carefully, noting sights, smells, feelings, ambiences before you return down the stairs, through the door to the everyday world.

This is a short and simple trip, but there are treasures to be gained by frequent visits to this storehouse of images. There is much for you to discover there, to understand an reveal into the light of new knowledge. You may even find hidden doors to other galleries, steps leading down to haunted inner rooms of other levels of consciousness where the stillness and the feeling of 'otherwhereness' is strong and definite. You might discover other Seekers there too, on quests of their own. You might find the maps of the mind-maze, or the Ariadne thread which brings you out of life's labyrinth, if you know what you are looking for. Take your time to get familiar with this crusty old place, for it is real. I know, for I have just come back from another visit.

It is really important that you are able to switch into the right state of consciousness for meditation and visualisation, and be aware of the difference in the way you feel and experience the world before you go on to the other, more complex techniques like astral travel or out of the body experiences, past-life recall or remote viewing, which used to be called travelling clairvoyance.

You must be able to shift level distinctly, time after time, and to retain the dual awareness on both levels, and to be able to return to ordinary waking consciousness immediately. This must be mastered before you try the more advanced arts, which will be discussed in later chapters. The last thing anyone wants in the magical world is for a novice Seeker to be blundering about in an uncontrolled state of mental confusion, seeing things which are not there, and being unable to sleep or properly wake up. Hasten slowly with these basic skills first and in time you will find a safe route through the hidden pathways of the mind.

CHAPTER THREE

The Circle of the Elements

The shape of the maze – as I learned from walking round – is hexago-
nal, with a pillar at each angle. Completing my circuit and arriving at
the entrance, I debated whether to go in; took a step or two; glimpsed
a passage a yard wide, running between hedges, and turning sharply.
Then the maze said NO to me.

Geoffrey Ashe, The Finger and the Moon

The use of a special place for the performance of magical or
religious rituals goes back a very long way. In some countries
these sacred spaces are still in use after thousands of years, in
others a new place has to be found to serve an ancient tradition.
In Britain there are many sites with sacred attributions, some
marked by Stone Age monuments, like Avebury, Stonehenge,
Callanish and Arbor Low, where earthworks and standing stones
mark out the arena, and whose antiquity seems to go back
beyond time itself. There are many other simpler sanctuaries,
often covered over by grand cathedrals or hilltop churches, in
city and remote countryside, which each served as a holy centre
for the area. Many are high on peaks or ridges, and usually the
most recent Christian foundation is dedicated to St Michael or St

George, those twin protagonists of dragons, who are but a more recent incarnation of the older sun and sky gods, worshipped in high places, with fire and dance. Traces of early sacred sites may be discovered in many West Country churches in their circular churchyard walls, often still showing ancient standing stones within their fabric, or where towering Celtic cross shafts shadow their porches, each still retaining its charge and power encoded by the ancient priesthood, and feeling like a tingle on the skin.

Many of the most sacred places were where natural phenomena were to be found, the ever-running spring clear and pure even in droughts, the lightning-struck tree with its black dead branches and green living ones. Great rocks shaped like the faces of gods and goddesses, deep pools, dark caves with their mystic stalactites and whispering subterranean streams, or the highest peaks of mountains where the stars might come to earth with their beams of energy, and glitter in the crystals of the hardest rocks, or sow the seeds of gold and silver underground. Deep in the shady groves of ancient forests which still persist in many places there are sacred sites, hidden dells where elementals and wood nymphs play on moonlit nights, and many wild creatures live, protected by the many-legged tree spirits whose power is great, and whose secrets are old and untainted.

Anywhere where two elements meet: earth and air; water and earth; air and water; or earth and fire – provides a sacred interface. Most of these are obvious outdoor locations like the edges of the sea and land, high in the hills, near lakes or waterfalls, but the last is the domestic hearth, the original centre of the homestead. Even today people still use the mantlepiece as a kind of altar, placing on it favourite ornaments, photographs of loved ones, and even candlesticks ready for any power cut. It is important to acknowledge the sanctity of a particular place and be able to recognise the subtle atmosphere which differs from a similar unblessed place, even if it is one corner of a bedsitter or the attic of a mansion or an ancient church or Stone-Age ritual site.

The paradox of magical circles is that they are usually marked out by a square! It appears to be a very old practice of marking the four points of the compass and then drawing a circle round these, but retaining something to indicate each direction. In some ritual systems there are elaborate sets of correspondences for each quarter, and it is necessary to invoke the presences of an archangel, wearing particular colours and carrying a certain ritual object at each corner of the ritual circle. Each lodge or tradition will have its own set of symbols, elemental weapons, colours, banners, officers, prayers, images and concepts relating particularly to the ceremony or inherited system, and there is no single set of agreed attributions! No way of applying the basic elements of your own working space is *wrong*, and ideally you will choose these as a result of much research, meditation and divine inspiration.

The underlying concept is that you have the Four Directions, north, east, south and west, and the Four Elements, earth, air, fire and water, so it is reasonable to allocate the one to the other. The actual problems start to arise when you try to decide which system of magical instruments you are going to add into the pattern, which usually involves a pentacle, pantacle, platter or shield; a wand, rod, arrow or lance; a sword, dagger, torch or lantern, and a cup, chalice, cauldron or bowl, depending on what you have, and the tradition or the group you are joining. You will need to think very carefully about each in turn and decide, or agree with those in authority, which will work best in the circumstances.

Not only are there the weapons, but on the altar itself it is common to find other representations of the Four Elements. These are sometimes items which can be consumed during a communion – for example, bread, cake or biscuits; wine, water or fruit juice; salt or honey; oil or milk; as well as incense or a flower for its scent; and some kind of lighted candle or nightlight or oil lamp. Clearly you can use earth for Earth, water for Water, fire for Fire and something airy for Air, but there is usually another layer of symbolism, so that Air, for example, is represented by a fan, or some feathers, or even a bell or horn that can be sounded. Once you start to look at these sets of four items the lists of possibilities become endless. It is well worth building up written tables with four columns for the elements, and working out sets of altar symbols, of instruments, colours, musical sounds, animals, plants, times of day and so on. Once you start you will find dozens of 'correspondences', as these related items are called, so that wherever you are, or whatever sort of ritual you might come to perform, you will always be able to find things which will stand for the elements during your working.

The reason for having this set of magical objects at the perimeter of your circle is that they represent balance. A wheel needs at least four spokes in order to be stable, and as you will see by looking at a bicycle, the more spokes the stronger the wheel. Each of the symbolic items is a spoke which is not only visible and tangible on this level of existence, but also on those more subtle planes of existence where the matters of magic have their own reality. As you will learn, it is important to be able to steer a straight and balanced course along the winding path through the magical maze. If you lean too far in any direction you will fall or be stopped by the nearest wall! Once you begin to understand the basic pattern of the circle with its four balancing points, you will have a secure and safe base to launch yourself off from. You might come to study the ancient Egyptian Tradition, where the Four Sons of Horus represent the directions; or witchcraft, where there are quarter candles, and the Mighty Ones of the Watch-towers are sometimes invoked; or Qabalistic ritual, where the Archangels, Uriel, Raphael, Michael and Gabriel guard the circle; or the Celtic tradition, with its four Totem Beasts. Whichever system you encounter, each has its sets of Guardians and Teachers whose presence is invoked at the start of a ritual. As you learn more you can add these sets to your tables, and discover which feel the most comfortable and interesting to you.

The magical circle is a place which is psychically cleared of any stray influences, usually by physical cleaning, and then by banishing any incompatible thoughts, and then by requesting the power or presence of whichever set of deities, symbols, elemental beings or images you wish, so that they protect the special atmosphere of the consecrated space. At the end you will need always to remember to thank these energies, even if you haven't sensed their actual presence, and bid them farewell. Whichever system you happen to use, you cannot *command* the Gods or Powers to attend you; you may only ask, because they are a lot bigger and more potent than any human being, and to order other aspects of creation about is both foolish and rude. How would you like to be commanded to appear in someone else's house and do their dirty work for them? Not at all, I would imagine, so don't ever try ordering other beings about, even if you don't believe in them! They are very real, on another level, and can get their own back by making your own life difficult if you upset them. You will have enough problems once you start to open up your inner levels of perception, so that you start to actually sense the different psychic 'vibes' which are around us all the time, though usually undetected.

You will need to learn to consecrate the symbols of earth, air, fire and water, and then by circling round with them, bless the area in which you are working. This works like invisible disinfectant so that distracting influences will vanish whilst you are performing your ritual, divination or healing, for example. At the end it is necessary to restore the natural atmosphere, for it is an often overlooked matter, that any banishment should be revoked because it cuts off *all* influences, including contact with your earthly friends. If you get into the habit of casting circles about yourself, day and night, you are likely to banish not only the minor distractions to magical work, but the love, affection and company of your family and friends. Banish too thoroughly and you rid your entire life of everything and end up in a psychic vacuum, with no friends or even animal company!

How you go about your consecration will depend entirely on your own religious feelings, your location and the sort of ritual you are doing. For example, if you are involved with a lodge of trained magicians then the banishing and consecration of the temple may be very elaborate, and then be followed by a 'composition of place', in which the magical scene is described and built up by all those participating. During this exercise the subtle change in level of consciousness shifts so that the created scene is more real than the room in which it is invoked. Some versions of this Opening Ritual, especially those written at the end of the last century, and still in use among more traditional ceremonial magicians, involve much equipment, incense, and the calling of names, or words of power. It can take over an hour, before anything else may take place, and much of it then has to be repeated at the end, to close down the energies, and return the participants to their ordinary mode of thinking. On the other hand, a simple, silent building of a ring of blue-white light around you as you sit down to meditate, taking a matter of seconds, can be perfectly adequate and do the job just as well.

The main objective of the cleansing and blessing of any place, in or out of doors, is to make it neutral to psychic awareness, so that just as you take a clean sheet of paper to write a letter, you can put into it exactly what you want or need, and nothing more. The blessing ritual is a sort of magical telephone number which attracts the attention of those angels, powers or elemental forces you need to come to your assistance, offer instruction, healing or accurate divination, and so on. Once you have called these beings up you must learn to be quiet and still and so hear what they have to tell you. It is no good launching into complicated ritual dances, gestures, chanting or drumming as you simply will not be able to receive whatever message those other orders of creation might have to say to you. How you perceive what they are communicating may well vary, from 'voices in your head', to pictures, to being fully aware of them as you would be of other people and scenery you encounter in the street. The more practice you have the easier it becomes, and the simpler the action of clearing and blessing the circle gets, just as familiar telephone numbers, no matter how long, are deeply embedded in your memory.

A magical circle is not only a two-dimensional ring, however, for we live in a four-dimensional world, with three dimensions of space and one of time, for the sake of argument. (There may be dozens of actual dimensions of space/time, but we are unable to detect these in our normal state of consciousness, although in certain magical states, this can be expanded somewhat!) The magical space is not only bounded by its square circle of the elements, but there is the dimension of up and down, and the central point, which, if you are on your own, is centred wherever you consider your seat of consciousness to be (think about that!), or at a point over the centre of the altar in a conventional lodge. This then gives you seven directions to bless, or request help from. You can add an eighth if you wish, for that is the outer circle which reaches to the edges of infinity and could be thought of as a limitless sphere.

It is customary, at the beginning of any working, simple or complex, to make yourself truly aware of these directions, using gestures, or carrying round elements or the instruments or symbols of the quarters, showing them both to your colleagues, if working in a group, and to the forces which will help your work. You will have to decide for yourself what goes where, and in which order these items will be presented. There is no one right way, and for a variety of reasons, any of them will work, so, like most of the basic arts of magic, you can't really do it wrong. What makes an occult action wrong is your frame of mind, attitude to the beings of other levels and your motives. If you demand immediate help, power or unreasonable assistance, you will most likely get a smack in the aura. Be polite in the world and most certainly when working any kind of magic, both to anyone you deal with, respecting their authority and position, and to any entities the rite might involve, whether you can sense them or not. Courtesy may be old-fashioned but it gets safe and effective results much more easily than shouting and demanding!

One of the most frequently encountered rituals is the Qabalistic Cross by which the magician blesses himself. He does this by touching his forehead and saying '*Ateh*', his solar plexus, saying

'*Malkuth*', his right shoulder, saying '*Ve Geburah*', and his left shoulder, saying '*Ve Gedulah*', and either putting his hands together or marking a circle through those points, saying '*Le Olahm*'. This is an ancient Hebrew blessing, found at the end of the Lord's Prayer, which in English is roughly, 'Thine is the Kingdom, the Power and the Glory for ever ...' often followed by Amen. There are lots of variations on this theme, and it is a matter of personal choice which feels right to you. The best version will be one you make up and use as your own signal that you are changing your focus from the apparent world to the magical one.

You will also need to mark out the invisible limits of your working space in all seven or eight directions, either by moving around the space marking your territory with the consecrated elements, or by words, sounds or gestures, not forgetting above and below, the central point, wherein burns the fire of the spirit (in temples traditionally represented by a living flame in a lamp), and perhaps the outer limits of the created universe. Do this in your own way slowly and sincerely. The one most important thing in magic is to take your time. Far more problems arise from rushed rites than from any other reason. Prepare all the things which you will need, put on your robe and regalia, if you wear them, allow your mind to become still and focused on the work, even if it is only a basic meditation. Preparation and calmness are never a waste of time. If you wish the ritual to occur at a particular hour, because the astrological positions of the planets are particularly beneficial at that moment, then allow plenty of time beforehand, especially if you are sharing the ritual with other people. You can never do anything in magic too slowly. You will find your nerves on edge, once you get into the swing of occult activity, and if you rush you will forget things and end up in a panic. The pressure of this work can be enormous and the only safe way to handle that power is slowly and carefully, allowing it both to build up step by step, and diminish at the end of the ceremony, step by step. With experience you will feel these positive changes taking place.

Allow yourself a space in the middle of even the most lengthy rite to rest and perceive what is going on about you, on all the levels you are able to comprehend. The more gently you take things the more gently you will find things happen about you, so you can see, hear and feel a wide variety of different things at once, and make the experience truly valid. This is just as important as dashing along, chanting words of power, calling upon

angelic forces, creating talismans and making elaborate gestures.
Most of the important aspects of magic are those pieces of new
information that are *received*, the *intuitive guesses*, the *solution
to a problem*, rather than your commands or requests to other
beings. The answer has to be of more use than the question!

A self-blessing ritual may be developed along the lines of the
following prayer, which is performed with appropriate gestures,
very slowly and sincerely, allowing each individual force to be
fully perceived before going on to the next direction:

From beneath me arises the energy of the Earth
my home and my foundation.

From above me pours down the power of the Sun
and the enchanting light of the Moon.

To my right hand comes the strength to control and direct,
the arts of magic.

To my left hand flows the skill to divine and to heal,
the source of blessing.

Before me arises the Perfected One I strive to become,
my magical True Self.

Behind me falls the one I was, and with it
all my discarded faults.

Around me circle the eternal stars,
lamps of wisdom in the deeps of space.

Within me grows the Flame of Light
the jewel of experience and arcane knowledge.

On me and my world may blessing be.

Allow the images of each part to arise within your inner eye. If
you are standing up at the commencement of any ritual, practise

with your eyes shut so that you don't fall over. This is a very potent invocation, arousing all the best aspects of your being, which you may not appreciate yet. Use this at the start of any working, meditation, ritual or any other magical work. It is not a banishing ritual, but an invoking one, calling from your own depths the strengths and powers to make your magic work. It needs to be learned by heart and each phrase meditated on, so that you really understand what is being requested. If you don't like these particular words, after due thought and contemplation, write your own 'Rite of Self-Blessing'. This is only one of the many simple ritual acts which you will need to discover, invent, or be inspired by the Gods to write. If you wear robes and regalia it is traditional to have a prayer for each item, blessing it and acknowledging its magical power.

You will need a short invocation to bless each of the Four Elements, which you then carry or show around the circle, depending on how much space you have, You need something to say to cleanse and sanctify that circle, and then to call into it the power, angelic force or deities you wish to work with, or consult for instruction. In most of the older books on magical arts you will find the Greater and Lesser Banishing Ritual of the Penta-gram, and of the Hexagram, and even the complete ceremony of Opening by Watchtowers, an extremely lengthy and complicated ritual, used by the Hermetic Order of the Golden Dawn, which uses the strange words of the Enochian Calls. This is very powerful stuff indeed, and should not be attempted without the direct guidance of an experienced teacher. No one is entirely certain of the origin of the Enochian language. Dr Dee, writing in the sixteenth century received some of it by a form of medium-ship, when Edward Kelley would scry in a crystal and Dee would write down what Kelley said he could see in the dark glass. This produced a series of diagrams and words and letters in a strange language. Dee thought it was the tongue spoken by angels in heaven, but other scholars have attributed it to ancient Atlantis, from which the roots of much Western arcane knowledge is drawn.

Once you have Opened or Cast the Circle it becomes a complete psychic barrier about your working place, and should be treated as such, even if at first you cannot feel or see it. You should never cast a circle and then wander in and out as if it was not there. Treat it as real, and so will any forces which you are dealing with. Inside the space will feel much larger, it will seem quiet, and there will be the tingle of anticipation in the air. It may also feel deserted and cut-off, if your banishing has been done thoroughly and sincerely. Different traditions will perform the ceremonial opening in different ways, some by having an officer of each quarter, invoking an Archangel and its elemental correspondences, while some witches light a candle at each point of the compass and draw a pentagram in the air, and then cleanse and seal the circle with consecrated water and salt. There are many variations on this basic pattern, which you will come across in the works of different traditions. They all work, and it will be best if you consider what you need to happen and then choose what you would like to do, as you progress through the maze of alternatives.

At the completion of any work, meditation, healing, divination or anything else, there is usually a communion of bread, salt and wine, and then the circle has to be closed by reversing the process from the beginning. Usually the quarter elements are thanked and the candles snuffed in the reverse order, and power is slowly and gently allowed to wind down. It is always important to allow plenty of time at the conclusion of any working to permit your state of consciousness to return absolutely to normal, for seriously performed rituals will cause a considerable variation in your level of consciousness to happen – if this doesn't occur you are not acting in a real magical way, merely acting! You will need to snuff any candles, throw out the hot ashes of the incense to the earth, take off your robes and put them away and write up the entry in your Magical Journal. Each of these things is important for it redirects your attention back to the everyday world. It is also well worthwhile having a hot drink and snack too, as this ensures you are fully back into your body. Recording the details of the ritual, its purpose and those participating is an important matter, too, as only by checking back over your records can you see what happened, how long a spell took to work, whether the divination was accurate, or in what manner the healing took place. Even the ideas which simple meditation generates are important for from these separate notions can gradually evolve entire new systems of knowledge and understanding.

To begin with you may well be perfectly content to use a little real earth, water, fire, and scents for air, but if you start to follow one of the more complex systems of ritual magic, or work witchcraft as described in any of the books based on modern traditions, you will discover that there are long lists of equipment, symbols, elemental weapons, statues, banners and personal regalia according to the source. Some of these items can be traced back to a book called *The Key of Solomon*, an ancient magical text which was published in the Middle Ages. It contains descriptions of all manner of strange rites; how to talk to spirits of the dead; how to become invisible; how to conjure the presence of angels; how to make talismans and perform acts of alchemy on base metals, or on your own psyche. These texts are many hundreds of years old, although many of them have been reprinted in modern books, but the methods really are old-fashioned and out of date. It is no longer necessary to sacrifice animals, or make blood offerings for any purpose. Sweet incenses work just as well as ox gall and toad spit!

The *Key of Solomon* also lists the tools and weapons which have come down, in part through fictional books and films, to the arts of modern practitioners. We don't really need swords and lances, daggers and burins, but some other safer, simpler and more appropriate symbols of the elements of air and fire should be found. Not only could it be embarrassing to be caught in the street with a three-foot sword, but it is illegal too. No one wants to end up in a police station rather than at a lodge meeting, so do be careful, if you choose to work with these old symbols. Explaining away a carrier bag of silver-plated chalices and dishes, a thurible on chains and some candlesticks to some over-worked policeman who has heard of recent thefts from churches will take more than magical skills and the art of invisibility! These may be trivial problems but they are real, and many experienced magicians have encountered them at one time or another over the last couple of decades.

If you only perform your ceremonies within the safe confines of your own home you may not run into such difficulties, but you still will have to buy or make your sword, the platter or pentacle of Earth, and a wand which can vary in length from a few inches to several metres. The Cup or chalice, goblet or cauldron should always be a gift of love, received by you unasked. If no one loves you enough to give you some symbolic token which can stand in for your magical cup, then the Goddess won't love you either! To be worthy and respected, loved and wanted is the only way to thread the maze of relationships between the human and magical levels. Love yourself, become worthy of loving, love others honestly and you too will be loved, and rewarded.

The practice of ceremonial magic, whether the seasonal and lunar orientated festivals of modern witchcraft, or the traditional elaborate rituals based on Qabalistic symbolism, written about by most of the well-known authorities, Eliphas Levi, Aleister Crowley, Gareth Knight and Dion Fortune, and many others requires a long list of regalia and equipment. Certainly if you have a lot of spare money you can simply send off to one of the occult suppliers for a 'Complete Temple Kit' for some fairly vast sum, or like the students who have spent many years of individual effort rather than cash, you can make, adapt and barter for all the items you need. Magically as well as financially the second option is by far the best. Magic works through links forged on the inner levels, and if you have spent many hours making, carving, embroidering or designing and painting some ritual object, it will be closely linked with you, and you will have marked it strongly with your own personality. The item might not be the most perfect of its kind, but it will be a potent symbol of your intention, and each time you see it, that subtle inner contact with the powers you hope to work with will be strengthened. If you do buy ready-made items they will be thoroughly steeped in the character of the maker, which will have to be wiped from the object by ritual cleansing, purification and then blessing. You will still need to imprint your own associations on the item as well. The same applies to anything you acquire second-hand.

Obviously some of the equipment is very hard to make, and this will offer you another turn in the labyrinth – do you follow the tradition which insists on a sword or dagger and a long lance or wand, or will you opt for an alternative solution, which hasn't been published in century-old sources? Because many of the objects symbolise something else – for example, the cup symbolises water, and may well contain water, you will have to choose what the cup is made of, bearing in mind its ritual use. In the old days most cups were solid silver, occasionally, gold, but later silver plate, as silver is the metal of the Moon and she rules the tides of the sea. Today the ritual cup is often made of glass, which is in fact, a liquid which moves only very slowly. Silver is silver in colour, but glass may be blue or green, clear or beautifully patterned, and glass goblets may be only the size of a wineglass for solo working, or enormous great chalices which need both hands to lift for group work. This is only one of the myriad problems of occult equipment that you will need to solve for yourself.

Putting aside the problem of a real temple, that is a room totally devoted solely to the practices of magic, divination and so on, you should study the following list of regalia, equipment, furniture and symbols to see just how much stuff could be required if you involve yourself fully in the magical arts. I doubt if this list is anything like comprehensive, either, and you will probably collect a large library of books on your particular interests as well!

To start with personal regalia, assuming you aren't going to work all your rituals totally naked ('sky-clad'), although in some traditions that is the way it is done (even then a necklace or belt or charm bag will be required), you will need a robe. These are usually full-length, hand-made and may be any colour, plain or embroidered, hooded, with long or short sleeves as you choose. The simplest is a long, narrow piece of cloth with a hole for your head, tied in round the middle with a cord or belt. The magical girdle is the second requisite; again it may be a particular planetary colour, or like those used in Judo, indicate your rank in a group, or personal achievement. Soft slippers are often worn if the floor is hard, although sandals are preferred in some traditions. Bare feet are all right but most people these days have very soft soles, so it rules out outdoor rituals in rocky places. Many groups have a symbolic pendant or 'lamen' worn on a ribbon or cord round your neck, again possibly showing your aspirations or position in a lodge. On your own it could be your zodiac sign, a hand-carved pendant of a god or goddess, or a painted/enamelled symbol which represents your ambition or the tradition in which you are training. You might fancy some sort of headgear, varying from a simple circlet of metal or a plaited gold elastic braid, to the Egyptian nemyss, made out of a square of silky material with one corner folded in to make a flat piece across your forehead, and held in place with elastic at the back. You could make a set of heads of the Egyptian or any other pantheon of gods or goddesses from carnival masks, or different coloured cloaks for the officers of the quarters, planets or signs of the zodiac. The list of possibilities is endless.

After you have sorted out what you will wear, and made it, for although you can buy robes, home-made ones are best, even if your stitching isn't very good (the bloodstains from pricked fingers will at least be your own!), you will need an altar. This can be a free-standing square table or upright cupboard, traditionally as high as a six-foot man's navel, in which you keep your equipment, or the top of a bookcase or shelf. If you can walk round it you will be able to perform more complex rituals, especially those which require blessing the elements and so on. The altar will need a series of covers, a black or dark purple undercover of heavy cloth or felt with tassels at the corners, then a white overcloth, perhaps with a lace or an embroidered edge. Sometimes a special coloured cloth is also used, to fit the correspondences of a particular ritual. Look out for large linen or silk hankies in the appropriate colours. You will also need silk cloths to wrap your Tarot cards or other divining gear in, to preserve their charge. The top of the altar can be covered with a sheet of plate glass as this prevents accidents from falling candles or tipped oil lamps and spilled wine.

You will also need a good solid chair to sit on. Some rituals can be very long, varying from twenty minutes of silent meditation to fully fledged, singing and dancing rituals, Gnostic masses, Enochian ceremonies and initiation rites which can last two to three hours! There are magical practices which go on all night, but if you are reading this book it is unlikely that you have come across that sort yet. The kind of chairs I have found most useful are either the old-fashioned wooden upright chairs with arms, which are called 'carvers' and used to grace the ends of the family dining table, or the much lighter, folding high-backed garden chairs. These should have a back tall enough to support your head and neck, for allowing yourself to slump during any magical work will be bad for your health, preventing easy breathing to continue, and even cutting off the blood to the brain if you let your head fall forwards and press on the carotid arteries. You might need some cushions in the small of your back, and something to rest your feet on, if your legs are short, because feeling secure when you relax into a meditation or ritual mental mode is very important.

You might also need a cassette recorder to play pathworking tapes on, or music during rituals, and also to record brief notes of what happened for your Magical Journal, which may be an audio one. This suggests the need for a power point or two, as you might require a small reading lamp near you, or any other electrical gadgetry which is appropriate to help your work. This can go on a small side-table, close to your chair, or if there are several of you, the Officer of Music, or Recording Angel, as designated.

On the altar you will need a central oil or nightlight lantern, usually with red or blue glass. You will need containers for the representations of earth, water, fire and air, and some actual water, rock, a candle and so on. You will need something to burn incense in, from the humble terracotta flowerpot filled with sand to a specially made chafing dish, a tile to stand it on, some blocks of special charcoal which light quickly, and a variety of sorts of incense to represent the flavour of the month, or purpose of the rite. The candlestick for fire, or whatever you choose to use, should be stable, and short candles should be used for safety's sake. You will, of course need matches, or perhaps for ritual use, the old-fashioned red-headed sort and a stone to strike them on.

For the communion you will need a platter for bread or biscuits, a dish for salt, and others for anointing oil, libations or any other runny substance, and a cup for the wine, water or fruit juice. You will also need a corkscrew dedicated to magical work so that you don't discover at the critical moment in a rite, when you need to pour an offering of wine, that you can't get the bottle open. This sort of thing spoils the whole atmosphere! Wine is also sometimes an added ingredient in incense, as are natural resins and honey, etc.

If your rituals are going to be elaborate ones based on the Qabalistic or Masonic tradition you will need two pillars. These may either be solid round pillars stood on firm bases (inner cardboard tubes from rolls of carpet are good and usually to be obtained free from skips, painted black and white), or they may be wide ribbons hung from the ceiling, or even collapsible pillars made of tubes of cloth supported by rings cut from plastic lemonade bottles – use your ingenuity. The pillars often have balls at the top of the capital. Wood, stiff cardboard or even discarded shop fittings can provide some very authentic looking materials if you paint and adapt them to your particular need. You can do wonders with polystyrene and a sharp knife or hot-wire kit.

For each quarter you might need a small table covered with an appropriate coloured cloth, a secure candle-holder or coloured lamp, and the particular instrument. This is where the platter, shield or pantacle comes in, for there is seldom enough space on the altar top to take large items, and quite often there are four people, each with their own robes, chairs and equipment, who represent the forces of the elements. You will also need the cup or goblet, which may be the same one used at the communion, and the sword, if used, or its subsitute, and for safety's sake, a solid

scabbard. Plastic swords may be symbolic, but magic requires
that each item is actually functional, so try to find or make a real
metal blade and hilt. It should have a sharp point or edge too, so
that it can function as a weapon of protection and power. The
fourth side requires the wand, or rod of power, which may be
decorated as a caduceus with wings and entwined twin serpents
(you can perform miracles with wire coat-hangers and papier
maché!), or a six-foot lance with a spearhead, or an arrow,
depending on which set of symbols appeals to you.

Some temples have a ritual floorcloth, painted to represent the
black and white squares of the Temple of Solomon, or with signs
of the zodiac or patterns to mark the positions of the elements, or
officers, or even a maze itself, to be slowly walked as a part of the
opening of the ritual. You might also be required to design and
make a banner with a symbol for the east and west of the lodge, or
a personal emblazonment to represent your magical aspirations.
You might have a cloak to wear over your robe; quite often this is
black or dark blue so that you can go out of doors for moonlight
rites, where the atmosphere is far more thrilling than that within
any four walls, no matter how consecrated.

Remember though, that these are stage props. They are very
valuable to any novice to teach the arts of ceremonial, the feeling
of wearing robes, of carrying a sword and making the salutes
with it, the sacred setting in which the tides of power can be
clearly felt to ebb and flow during the consecration and closing of
the working. It is a place outside of time, between the worlds of
reality and magical reality, and the training ground of all real
adepts. The hours of making, designing, planning and working
are all valuable. You will never achieve any power without them,
nor will you learn to use those subtle changes in mental focus in
which the worlds of magic become more real without many,
many hours of patient practice. Eventually you will grow out of
the need for these props, but it may take ten to twenty years! If
you develop skills and love of ritual you may never discard the
system at all. You will be able to work in the field of mind and
consciousness, but your inner self will be remembering the real
feel of the robes and instruments, the actual scents of incense and
candle wax, from which power derives.

CHAPTER FOUR

The Ways of the Gods

Here some loose ends may be tied up. The maze pattern has been
shown to represent 'Spiral Castle' or 'Troy Town', where the sacred
Sun-King goes after death and from which, if he is lucky, he returns.

Robert Graves, THE WHITE GODDESS

One of the other parts of the great labyrinth of magical knowledge is that of religion. Many people come to witchcraft or other
occult arts, not necessarily for the power aspect, but for the
religious freedom which many call 'paganism'. This is a particularly complex and entwined subject, for as a little study will
show, most of the groups or pantheons of gods and goddesses are
imported from somewhere else. A quick look round the Ancient
Religions section of a public library will show beautiful pictures
of the gods of Ancient Greece, the animal-headed deities of
Dynastic Egypt, the vast ramifications of the Hindu pantheons,
or the stern faces of the Classical gods and goddesses of Ancient
Rome. Their titles and attributes are explained, their myths
expounded, their symbols depicted, yet nowhere are there clear
instructions as to how or where they might be reached in this day
and age. The Celtic and Ancient British gods remain, as ever,

invisible, unnamed and silent in their groves of sacred trees and beneath the unhewn dolmen of their oracles. To find them requires the threading of the most immanent yet most puzzling of mazes, for though the gateway is always before our faces we cannot see it unless we have the token of these local deities in our hand, and the desire to encounter them in our hearts.

To 'become a pagan' is the objective of many who set forth on the paths of magic, yet few really consider that they may be casting off the old shackles of one established religion to take up the heavy chains of another. The gods of any tradition are not just names; they are not like vast toys which can be brought forth, played with, and then discarded in a dark cupboard when not required. They exist in their own levels of Creation, they have powers of which we of earthly inheritance can have only the slightest inkling. They are absolutely real and we should all be well aware of this when we seek them out. It doesn't much matter whether your flight from the cruel Jehovah is to the older Jove, God of Laughter; or from the love of Jesus into the arms of Venus, Goddess of Love, but you will have to undergo the initiation of culture-shock. The Old Religions do not place the buffer of priests between worshipper and worshipped, they lead you down through the dark passages of ritual and cast you alone and unprepared into the blazing light of the epiphany of the Gods themselves.

The words 'pagan' and 'heathen' mean 'countryman', so you will see at once that if you are an urban soul it will be necessary for you to venture into the wild places where the Gods of nature dwell. You will need to go through these places in reality, so that the keys of them may be found and carried back into your own sanctuary where they may reopen the gates to those sacred lands where the deities are to be found. There is a direct road which has to be trodden by each Seeker for himself, for the Gods have to be encountered directly, seen and their presence felt. It is an awesome experience for one accustomed to the pleasant atmosphere of a church or chapel, where for the most part, you are merely a spectator at the service. In orthodox religions the mystery is experienced by the priest alone, and is not shared with the congregation. In magical religious rituals the opposite is true. You become the priest, understand the Mystery and participate fully in the presence of the Gods and the communion between all levels of being. Very rarely do magical priests serve the congregation, where there is one; usually they serve the Gods, and the

elements of the ritual communion are passed from one partici-
pant to the next, each bestowing his or her blessing and passing it
on, from the most senior to the most junior.

You will have to recognise that there are a variety of beings of
other levels of creation, from the Creator or First Source down-
wards. Some of these will be the actual pantheons of gods and
goddesses, some will be angels and archangels, some will be
powers or elemental spirits, which, contrary to common folklore, are not small creatures like garden gnomes, but vast ephemeral forces linked with particular elements, and other non-visible
forces. These beings *are* visible if you shift your consciousness to
their level, which is why mastering the art of meditation is so vital
to any magical act. It is hard enough dealing with creatures from
the inner worlds without further complicating the process by not
even being able to see them and receive messages through gesture,
setting and appearance!

Most of the gods or angels are shaped as *we* imagine them to be,
not as they really are in their own worlds. We have set images to
which they conform so that we can recognise them, by the clothes
they wear, the symbol they carry and so on. We have imposed
false filters and lenses which reflect an illusory image to our
limited human vision. If we have the courage and determination
we can learn to encounter all the gods and goddesses as *they are*,
within their own chosen settings. That is why there has always
been a magical priesthood, who with unveiled sight, has had the
daring to consult the Old Gods, asking for oracles, for strength
and for wisdom. The tradition tells that Isis, the great Goddess of
the Egyptian pantheon, is always seen veiled. It is humanity who
have imposed the veil, not the Goddess. We don't have priests
outside the innermost magical temples who have been trained to
encounter the deities direct. Should any of them appear during a
ritual, the unprepared participants are quite likely to faint with
shock!

In the old days the priests transmitted the messages of the will
of the Gods to the people, speaking in parables and simple stories,
but they could equally well lead the initiates through the doors of
consciousness by their arts, to come face to face with the Old
Gods for themselves. Some people have never sought this path,
preferring their religious experiences watered down and
explained to them rather than undergoing the awesome process of
personal revelation. In the age to come this may well change, and
a new priest and priestesshood spring up to re-establish the

ancient link between worshipper and deities. To be a poet, priest and king were the three attributes of the Chosen Ones. The Goddess herself would grant the poetic ability through divine inspiration, the priesthood had to be gained by functioning as a priest by revealing the messages of the Gods to the people, and the right to rule was also granted by the inner levels. There was a true unity of mind and spirit within the sacred person of the ruler. Today vestiges of the ritual of instilling this divine link are retained in the coronation ceremony of modern monarchs. Anointing makes one a Christ, for that is what 'christ' means, one anointed with chrism. Anointing is retained in many initiation ceremonies for this reason, so that the initiate becomes blessed and able to function as an anointed one, if he is properly trained to perform this onerous task.

Every Seeker will have to decide for himself what sort of god, or gods and goddesses he will work with by examining what he knows and expanding his religious experience by approaching these deities in their own realms through meditation and both outer and inner journeys. There is no short-cut, and it is vital to stick to one path at a time. This might sound obvious but a glance through many of the modern books containing pagan rituals will show the participants invoking deities from many mixed, and often mutually conflicting pantheons. It is not safe. The Gods are real and separate. Just because the Greeks, Romans, Egyptians and Celts had a goddess with a particular attribute, for example a Moon Goddess, it doesn't mean they are all the same goddess. That is a mistake often made by students of Qabalah, for they tend to use the Tree of Life as a universal filing system, and imagine, through lack of personal experience, that all gods are the same. Dion Fortune may have written 'All Gods are one God, and all Goddesses are one Goddess, and there is one Initiator' but it doesn't mean all gods *are* the same! What she was saying was that all deities are *aspects* of One Creator, which being huge like a mountain, may be perceived as different facets by a Seeker trudging through the foothills below. There is *one* mountain but many ways of approaching it, and many ways of seeing it, all different and all valid, but none of them total.

Most Seekers are familiar with what they take to be names of gods and goddesses, in any given pantheon, but again, this is not as simple as it seems. What we suppose to be names are, in fact, descriptive titles. Some of these have no clear interpretation to us. Take the Egyptian goddess Isis. Her actual name was Aset and that means 'throne'. Now how do you get from that to the various attributes of this great goddess, usually seen as both Moon goddess and as Earth Mother? It isn't for me to say, but through meditation on the Moon rising from a calm sea, like the glorious description given by Lucius at the end of Apuleius' book, *The Golden Ass*, you might have a true vision of the Goddess, who will surely explain herself to you, as she has done to her worshippers for thousands of years.

Whichever tradition you choose to work with first will need to be examined in this light. Each god has a title and by building around the symbolism that title throws up, you will come to know each for yourself. The magical way of religion is and has always been by personal revelation, by knowledge, not blind faith. Experience does not need a false structure of other people's opinions to hold it up in the light of personal comprehension. Everyone is free to meet the Gods on their own terms, ask questions direct and receive whatever answers he is capable of understanding. You have to make the effort to achieve that meeting, through ritual, prayer, vigil or whatever seems to be the most likely way through the maze of personal contact. You then won't need to believe what someone else says, you will know for yourself. Don't take my word for it, seek out a god or goddess, an elemental or angel for yourself, and see what I mean.

What is most important is that you become fully aware of the whole of a particular tradition before mixing it in with any other. Adepts can work with a variety of different pantheons because they are able to keep them separate by entering a different level of consciousness for each, but novices should, for their own safety, stick to one pantheon alone. You also need to be aware that because changes took place among the people whose Gods you are working with, new pantheons were introduced, and in many places new 'families' of gods and goddesses took over from the set before. These *are not the same* with different names, they are a new collection of deities. Ra is *not* Aten, who is *not* Osiris, for example. Each of these is a god from a different pantheon and they must not be confused. Read the stories and legends, and most important, make plans or charts of the relationships. In one Egyptian pantheon, for example, this is quite complicated. Isis is Osiris' wife but also his sister. Nephthys is her sister and is married to Set, Osiris' brother, but is later married to Anubis. Horus, the son of Isis and Osiris, was conceived after Osiris had been killed by Set. The other main deities in this collection include Anubis, Hathor, Thoth, Sekhmet and Bast. Each has his or her particular attributes, legends and magical or religious duties. There are many excellent illustrated books which explain the stories of the different pantheons of Egyptian gods, showing the details of their heads and headdresses which show what each was concerned with. You must spend a lot of time coming to understand fully why the Egyptian Gods are shown with the heads of animals. Their bodies and hands are human, although many of the statues are huge, but their faces or headdresses represent animals or birds. It is a key to the whole Mystery system, and warrants long meditations and inner journeys to the Temples of the Nile to understand these matters. If you wish to work Egyptian magic there is an excellent book by Murry Hope called *Practical Egyptian Magic* which is a very good starting-place, and she also wrote *Practical Greek Magic*, which explains the gods and goddesses of the ancient Greeks. Many systems of magic, from the ancient Atlantean to the American Indian, incorporate the idea of the squared circle. In the Egyptian tradition, for example, the circle may be guarded by the Four Sons of Horus, who are protectors in life, and after death were set to take care of the inner organs of the body of the mummified pharaoh or priest. Like their hawk-headed father, each has the mask of a different creature; Imset has a human head, Hapy the head of an ape, Qebensenuf the face of a falcon and Duamutef the head of a jackal. Each of these gods is guardian of a particular direction, and so acts as keeper of the circle, if you wish to work with this system.

You will need to learn the difference, in any tradition, between gods, messengers and heroes. This applies particularly to the Celtic tradition for here the deities certainly don't have names; they all have titles or descriptive phrases, by which they are commonly known. If you are not familiar with the Celtic languages you will not know what any of their 'names' mean, and as most of them will appear only as symbols, seen vaguely through the misty atmosphere of these Western lands, you will find it hard to decide who you are dealing with. You will need to begin with the heroic tales from the Irish, Scottish or Welsh past. Each of these encompasses a vast collection of stories, genealogies and poems which existed only by word of mouth for thousands of years, and were only written down between the sixth and twelfth centuries AD. Many of them were not translated from their original Celtic tongue until the last century, so there is a great body of unstudied material gradually becoming available as scholars provide modern translations, and those with deeper insight are able to unravel the Mystery within. In the Welsh stories known as the *Mabinogion*, for example, there are the seeds of the whole initiation process of the individual, known as the 'Mabon', the child, who undergoes a variety of transformations, journeys, imprisonments and adventures and gradually becomes a poet, hero and wise man. Some of the stories involve King Arthur and his Knights, and this links in with real history, although the themes of quests for sacred or mysterious objects hidden in the Otherworld certainly date back long before the sixth century, Arthur's 'historical' time.

In the Celtic tradition the gods and goddesses are much more human, they make mistakes, fall in love, wreak revenge, set up and solve riddles and overcome disadvantages. There are very tangled skeins of different clans of gods taking over from earlier ones, and there are human heroes who trace their descent from one of the goddesses. The basic system is matriarchal, and each realm is ruled by a queen who gains her power from her mother. Her husband rules as king only because he is her husband. In this framework there are human magicians, some of them of more than human stature, like Merlin, who under one name or another, in disguise or under enchantment, appears and reappears throughout the whole of the Welsh and Scottish tradition, in tale and song, in poem and picture. Although he is not a god he has many powers which make him like a god, and he guides the underlying story of magic, initiation, kingship and quest through all its stages. Even today his presence can be felt and his voice heard, and the legends which surround his life and times are not forgotten.

Many aspects of the lives and religious practices of our ancestors are really only being understood for the first time, often many thousands of years after they have ceased. Historians had little evidence to go on in the non-literate lands of the North, where writing the sacred texts was forbidden, and the cultivation of memory, the use of poem and song, tale and chant was the way in which information was preserved and passed on to the next generation. Much of the way we think about the ancient people of Britain, for example, has come down to us from their enemies, the powerful and literate Romans, who for over four hundred years, tried to unite the clans, and change the ways of life and worship of the people here. They feared the magical power of the shamans, believing every second Briton was some sort of witch or wizard, and feared the ruling authority of the Druid priests, which held the fractured society together by law and religion. Although these learned astrologer-priests had several written languages it was through verses committed to memory that their teaching endured. The Ogham alphabet was only used on gravestones to record the names and deeds of the deceased, resting under the cairn, or for occasional boundary markers, not for records or books as we would know them today.

All the ancient traditions kept their most sacred magical and religious matters in their heads, passing them on only to initiates who were bound with oaths of silence. Many of these oaths were never broken and so much of the inner aspects of the Mysteries, the names of the gods and goddesses, the rites of the priests and the training in magic of the initiates has remained forever hidden in the mists of antiquity. It is through those woven and over-grown paths that any new Seeker must make his way, often running into the guardian thorn thickets of the Otherworld wherein the secrets of magic lie hidden to this day. Sometimes you will encounter blind ends, deep in the caves of mystery, sometimes arrive at a high point where a view across a wide and forested landscape stretches to the sea's glittering horizon, but no path leads through the wilderness until you make it!

The secrets of the past priesthoods have been carefully con-cealed, but they were never destroyed. Some small fragments have come down to us even today, and can be found as computer 'Dungeons and Dragons' games, or in books, folk-songs, tales and poems. The idea of the Quest, in which the Seeker leaves his home and the way of life his family wish him to follow, and where he braves strange lands, meets odd characters, encounters dan-gerous situations, and is eventually rewarded, underlies many of the oldest legends. These concepts might seem archaic but they hold good even now. If you want to take up the magical path, you will have to go through a similar journey, leaving behind the known way and conventional ideas. You will encounter strange people, peculiar theories, symbols and myths, and from them glean the seeds by which magical power is gained. If you persist, working in dream and meditation, in inner journey and personal research among the ruins of the lost traditions as you find them to this day, you are sure to uncover the keys which will unlock parts of the hidden and forgotten past.

You will have to decide which tradition you are going to

explore and read all you can about the gods and goddesses, their symbols, the things they did, their interaction with other gods and mankind. Each is a separate, eternal force, still existing in another level of reality. By working with the things you learn you can reanimate their landscapes, rebuild their temples in the inner world, reinvoke their Mysteries, learn to sing again their praises, use the invocations which ask for aid, for healing or for instruction about the future. You can make real the fabric of your inner vision; it will build with mind bricks the sacred places of the past, be they stone or wood, grove or palace. You will be able to enter there with the right gestures of worship, to give thanks and to make requests, to seek the answers to questions and to perform arts of divination and magic. The ancient gates have been restored, and the keys are available to anyone who has the patience, courage and will to find them. The oldest gods have never withdrawn from our world, we have retreated from them behind the false barriers of uninspired religious teaching and solid dogma. The words and writings of men have overscored the sacred texts inscribed on the face of the Earth, and in the sky among the stars. We have forgotten to look to the light of the Sun and Moon for guidance, preferring the easier forms of man-made intelligence, and mundane not sacred guidance.

We will have to learn again that the ancient peoples, all over the planet, did not worship the Sun and Moon for themselves, but as givers of Light, as symbols of a greater force for which these visible stars and planets were just God-created things on which to focus prayer or request. The Old Religions are based upon nature and take for their holy places and sacred images nothing which has been made by the hands of man, but trees, springs of fresh water, the flight of birds, and the distant gleam of travelling stars. For the most part their holiest sites were on high hills and mountain peaks, where the feet of the Gods in the sky might touch the world. Even the specially constructed places had holes in the roof and walls where the light of the sun or moon or certain stars might penetrate at the height of the Mystery. Even in rain-soaked Britain, famous for fogs and clouds, the most ancient sacred enclosures are marked with banks and ditches and standing stones but do not appear to have ever had roofs on.

Through thoroughly immersing yourself in the legends of your chosen pantheon you will become very familiar with the symbols of each of the deities, knowing which one carries a bow, a lance or a caduceus, and which is associated with horses or birds, has a

sacred cauldron or the shepherd's crook. Gradually this will start
to make sense to you, and you will be ready to approach the Gods
in their own lands to ask favours, to give thanks for gifts
received, or enquire from their oracles about what is to be. This is
a slow process, but it is important to get it right. If you have
grown up in an orthodox religion, what you will learn from
invisible sources is very different from the dogma of the Bible and
the Church, for it will come in the form of personal experience.

As has been said before, the magician does not *believe*, he
knows from individual revelation. Faith is a scaffolding put up
around some very shaky concepts which will not stand up
without it. If you take away faith the edifice of orthodoxy might
well crumble into dust. If the religion is based on personal
communion with the Gods there is no faith to crumble, but sure
knowledge and genuine experience, subjective though it may be,
but totally real and solid to those who have been through it. By
actually meeting and conversing with the deities, participating in
their communions, gaining knowledge, healing or direction from
them at source, you will come to realise that they are aspects of
Creation within the reach of human consciousness, not remote
Gods set far beyond the ken of humanity, and whose words have
to be brought back by the mediation of a priesthood.

Great changes are taking place in religion at present. The
Church is having to prepare for the ordination of women. The
Jewish religion already permits lady rabbis in some traditions.
The whole matter of priestly calling and the function of the
mediator between heaven and earth is coming under close
scrutiny, and sending rumbles of alarm through the Establish-
ment. If the Church were aware how many priests and priestesses
are already functioning within the pagan framework, all round
the world, it might make them very alarmed. There is a place for a
priesthood for there will always be some people who need to
follow and cannot face revelation and religious experience for
themselves. There is a need for the voices of the Gods to be
reported to the people, and their will explained in ordinary
human terms. There is a natural longing to be able to worship, to
share communion, to acknowledge gifts and to request guidance
or practical help. There is a need for counselling, for personal
spiritual advice and comfort in times of trouble or despair.

It is quite likely that a new form of religion will come into being
in the years to come, when many of the different aspects of what
is now thought to be 'pagan' are amalgamated with the *status*

quo. The pagan, for want of a better word, accepts the idea of karma, the action and reaction which takes place at a spiritual level. This is very different from the Christian concept of punishment and reward, sin and forgiveness of orthodox faiths. In mystical terms, if you make a mistake, you are responsible and it is up to you to redeem yourself, by restoring what you harmed. Responsibility is personal, and cannot be usurped by some priest, nor can anyone else offer forgiveness and by sacrifice, redemption to another. If you make mistakes you will have to put them right, if not in this life, then in the next. You cannot live a cruel and selfish life and expect to get off scot-free because you have confessed your sin to another person. Half the people in the street seem to go around weighed down with the burden of sin because they cannot obtain forgiveness without confession, and they are not able to confess. In the magical tradition, you only need to admit your failure to yourself, and to the immortal Gods, not to receive absolution, but to be given guidance as to how to put right what you made wrong. You must examine every action you make, admit your faults at least to yourself, and deal with them. You must cope with personal guilt feelings, not by getting someone else to bless them away, but by actually striving to repair what was harmed. Often this is impossible, but the Lords of Karma who ensure that the balance is kept true, in cosmic terms, will offer you an appropriate chance to correct the past and put right, in some other way, those things out of line.

If, as is accepted in most magical, pagan and non-orthodox Christian religions, you live many lives, you will be certain to get chances of rebalancing the books, as time passes. When you have been harmed by the deeds of others you will receive restitution. It doesn't appear to work on literally a tit-for-tat basis – in other words, if I harm you in this life, you will harm me an equal amount next time round, but rather the harm I have done will occur through the agency of some third party in the future. The working of the karma can often be observed, and frequently the people who are convinced they are under psychic attack by some evil magicians are simply on the receiving end of some of the nasty things they have wished or performed on others during this, or some other, life. You will need to explore all these concepts for yourself. Look at the idea of sin and forgiveness, and the nature of penance and absolution in the terms in which you learned of these things, and in the light of reincarnation and karma. Think about the true function of a priest, and the need for many of the duties performed by the priesthood down through the ages, which in its very eroded form is seen in the churches of today. Consider the ideas of communion, of sacrifice and offering, of redemption and restitution. Try to discover how karma has worked in your own life, and that of the lives of people around you.

In the past the priest had a number of different functions to those he has today. When the Christian Church won out over the Druidic religion, many of the Druidic arts were absorbed into the Celtic Church. These were later thrown out by the Church of Rome in the sixth century. There were druidesses who acted as oracles, receiving direct inspiration, in sacred caves or enclosures, from the ancient gods. Both the druids and druidesses were healers with plants, by laying on of hands, and through incubation, the magical, hypnotically induced sleep wherein dreams gave clues to cures. Like priesthoods in other lands, they could handle snakes with impunity, and converse with animals. Their ritual sacrifice was of a white bull, just as it was in many distant places, from Crete to the North American plains. On the skin of the bull the priests would sleep and receive visions and views of the future. They were law-givers and keepers of mundane justice, and executioners of the convicted murderer. They made ritual images of the gods of nature, and cast them upon fires or into the sea to ensure luck and fertility of crops and fishing and people. They would act as teachers and recorders of history, not on parchment, but in the subtle and indelible records of the trained mind which could recite a hundred poems, each lasting a day, and tell you the whole history of the world! They made music, verses, and would sing a satire against their enemies which would make them tremble with fear. They would learn the names of the gods of rival tribes and cry them out over the scenes of battle, thus reducing the enemy to faintness and shame. They could raise winds and storms at sea, and mists, and cause the sun to stand still on earth, and much of their hidden heritage still lives with us in the arts and magics of the village witch, the shaman and the dowser.

Each family or clan would have its totem beast, its ritual tree and sacred animal which it was forbidden to kill or eat at feasts. The records within the memories of the Bards would include all these taboos, and the restrictions or sacred tasks laid upon anyone as the result of a challenge, for often the Celts would set up a puzzle rather than a fight, and whole kingdoms could be lost over a board game which pre-dates chess, called Fichel or Tavl. The deeds of heroes who were the clan's ancestors would be sung around the communal hearth, and any new exploits in battle or love, in chariot-racing or cattle-thieving would be added to the repertoire of the oral tradition. Some of those ancient songs and lays are with us yet, in the convoluted tales of folklore and ballads. You can recover your own totem beast and the magical symbol of your clan, if you can work your way back through the undergrowth of the Celtic wilderness, whose paths have been long overgrown and lost. You will have to find a way through the thickets of sacred trees, and carve out a path among the old forest where the deer run, and the bats fly, and the ghosts of long-forgotten dragons breathe fire into the twilight world. It is a strange realm, so close and yet so well concealed, but any who seek out the Old Gods of the Celtic Tradition will need to venture there, and in the dim-lit dells, rediscover the Gods of Pool and Tree, of the Underworld and the Sun, or the Horse Goddess and her birds, or the Sow Goddess and her sacred cauldron. You may find remnants of the cult of the head, or of the gods who fly through the air, who die or are sacrificed as the Corn King, to be reborn around Yuletide. You will discover that goddesses may change their form from young virgin to aged crone, but they never die. There is a Mystery here for those who can unravel it.

Under the vague heading 'folklore' or 'folk tales' you will find many traces of these ancient Mysteries, from all parts of the world. They are the last remnants of the priestly teaching, at first explained and handed out to the initiates, and the adherents of various ancient religions, which gradually filtered through into he popular songs, tales, poetry and traditions of their respective ages. Many folk customs which survive even in Britain today may have their roots firmly embedded in rituals for fertility, protection or petition dating back many thousands of years. Any book on 'Calendar Customs' will show what sort of rites were celebrated when. A few sessions of meditation, or Goddess-inspired guesswork, may well lead you to understand the significance of round yellow cheeses, or round yellow pancakes and the Sun's return. The connection between spring flowers, candles, chicks and eggs may become clear, and the link between bonfires, apples, mirrors, masks, Hallowe'en and death emerge from the winter fogs if you apply magical common sense to the matter.

You will need to consider the whole concept of life, death, the afterlife, reincarnation, karma, and how best to pursue your own spiritual development, within an orthodox or 'pagan' religious framework. It is not a thing to ignore, for the true rewards of magical excellence and competence are not paid in cash, but in terms of spiritual awareness and evolution. You will know that you cannot take material wealth into the afterlife, but any gains made on the spiritual road will go with you through the pattern of reincarnations. This is not an unrealistic sort of 'holier than thou' attitude but a practical awareness which underlies your relationships with people, it provides the motives for acting in particular ways, how you deal with difficulties and problems. It will act as a conscience, a link with your Holy Guardian Angel, who is always with you, protecting and guiding whenever it gets the chance. You may well develop a true bond with this facet of your eternal soul, being well aware of the rights and wrongs as you encounter them in the world.

For all these subtle, spiritual steps there is no convenient formula, no handy rite to perform and immediately assure knowledge and conversation with your Holy Guardian Angel, as it is expressed in the book of Abramelin the Mage. It is hard work, like anything worth doing; it takes time, commitment and patience. You need to be able to perceive the non-material aspects of much of the magical work you may come to do. You will need to be guided by these inner, eternal forces, whether you are performing a simple divination, or a healing ritual, or asking for assistance and direction. The more you work with each of the inner worlds – that of the gods and goddesses, that of the elementals and those of the spiritual levels within yourself – the more certain you will be of the way you are supposed to go through the labyrinth of life. Help is always available, but you do have to ask for it. Study and meditate on these matters and you will gain a close and fast-acting link so that you only have to frame a request or petition in your mind and an answer will come to you, either mentally, or in the words of someone you speak to, or in the pages of a book, on TV, or in any medium. The gods are quite capable of adapting modern technology to provide the answers, if you have the wits to look at ordinary sources of information, instead of sitting in a magical circle, cut off from reality, waiting for an archangel to turn up with your desire on a velvet cushion. If you insist on that approach you may be in for a long wait!

If you want to get to know the gods and goddesses of your chosen pantheon (and I really do advise you to choose one and tick to it, at least for a year or two!), steep yourself not only in the various stories about them, but if possible visit their landscapes. If you choose Rome or Egypt or Greece, or somewhere further away than these, you may not be able to go there often, but you can get well-illustrated books, slides and coloured posters which will evoke a little of their atmosphere. If you are looking to the Old Gods of Britain you will need to explore the wild places, untouched except by wind and weather. You might discover them in forests, on moorlands, in caves and along the coastline on stormy days. It will be a lonely pilgrimage, but the cost in time and personal discomfort is a small price to pay for that permanent and living link between you and the worlds unseen by ordinary folk. Once you have been to their domain and genuinely experienced them, encountered their power and particular energies, you will be able to bring that response into the safe confines of your own home or temple. You cannot command their presence, they are far greater than you, but you can open a channel of communication, make ready somewhere to receive them, and if they consider your request valid, they will come. This applies equally to 'pagan' deities as it does to orthodox Christian ones. You can meet and talk with Jesus and the Disciples, just as you can call on Artemis or Bran. Accept that each is real, be willing to make that sacrifice of ordinary consciousness to enter their worlds, be thankful and respectful, and you will add a new dimension to your life.

There are a number of different spiritual or religious tasks anyone following a New Age path will need to understand, whether they are in a position to join a working group or coven, or seek for enlightenment alone. First, how do you intend to work with the gods and goddesses you have chosen? Do you wish merely to perform rituals from someone else's book to worship deities you do not know very much about, or do you want to build up your own selection of Seasonal Festivals, each celebrating a part of the natural yearly cycle of birth, fruition, death and rebirth? Are you prepared to make lonely overnight vigils in some secluded place, far from the glow of the city lights, where the spirit of Pan or the Morrigan can come and scare the wits out of you? How about a week of religious and magical work, asking for different kinds of guidance each day, using the symbolism of the planetary deities, in your chosen pantheon? In the Catholic faith there is the Novena, nine days of dedication and prayer, usually asking for healing or divine guidance.

There is a long history of the concept of Communion, a shared ritual meal of bread and salt and wine, in the Old Religion, although modern witches have a feast of Cakes and Wine, or even four-course dinners during their ritual celebrations. You might, at this point, consider the sacrifice of animals for food and clothing. Can you tolerate the taste of dead meat from some slain beast, or would you prefer to eat only the fruit of the tree and life of the corn? If you do become a vegetarian (and some occultists advise the aspiring magician against this), you will have to learn how to stay healthy, what you need to eat each day so that you don't suffer deficiencies of any sort. In the occult world you may encounter vegans who eat no animal products of any kind, and as hospitality might require you to offer them a meal, you ought to know what they may eat and what not. The same applies to religious Jewish or Muslim people who may have not become 'pagan' but adhere to their own country's dietary laws.

In the fictional literature of magic much is made of sacrifices of animals, and pouring of blood upon the altars of the ancient Gods, but this is left over from long ago. In Classical times nearly all gods and goddesses were offered the life and blood of particular animals, from the doves sacrified to Venus, to the sacred bulls slain in honour of many gods across most of the world. Today we still make dedicated sacrifices, but of our own time and energy. We offer sweet-scented flowers and incenses, joss-sticks and vaporising perfumes. We offer our years of study and from these we are rewarded by gaining knowledge and power and the certainty that the Gods are near us, that they hear and often answer our prayers. This is a real experience which only comes from daring to approach the Gods direct.

Another set of problems which might come to bother you once you establish your desire to be a pagan, or at least follow some arcane or antique form of religion, is that of weddings, funerals and baptisms. Orthodox faiths have specific services to celebrate the birth of a child and a ritual to name it, accept it into that religious community, they have wedding services and those for the dying and departed. In some branches of the pagan world, particularly in America, where witches can register as priests, rituals can be conducted to fulfil these various situations and the results are legal. In Britain there is no acceptable pagan marriage rite, and those who want to be 'Hand-fasted', to use a gypsy tradition which many witches have adopted, have to marry at a

Register Office and then get their coven's High Priest and High Priestess to carry out the pagan wedding ceremony. Certainly, if you are arranging for a friend to be cremated, the crematorium will permit any kind of service, so long as it doesn't last too long. You can simply choose sacred music and pray in silence for the repose of the deceased, or you can burn incense in small quantities and sing his praises, dance even, so long as you arrange it first. But, more often than not, the family and relations are orthodox members of some other church and would be appalled at the idea of pagan celebrations, feasting and music in honour of the departed. It may be easier to adhere to orthodox burial rites and have your own private memorial ritual and feast later on.

Another matter related to this is making a magical Will. Almost everyone who is seriously involved in the study and practice of magic will acquire a great deal of equipment, books, magical diaries and robes over the years. This is not the sort of collection which should casually be disposed of by non-initiated members of the family. It is *vital* that a letter should be clearly written which states your personal wishes about a pagan funeral, if you really want one, and the names of several people who should be contacted and asked to dispose properly of any magical papers and consecrated weapons and regalia. You need to give several names because it might be many years before it is necessary to carry out your last wishes. Another approach would be to leave the address of the Pagan Funeral Trust,* or, if you are a solo worker, the address of one of the most reputable occult magazines, because all of the better ones will have people who know about the proper way to treat magical objects and equipment. Although in the past it was traditional that all personal magical papers, diaries and the like were burned on the death of the initiate, today, because these papers can contain much valuable information for those who come afterwards, it is far better that all your journals and notebooks are taken into the care of a society or group who will treat them properly, storing them in a library for later consultation by other initiates on the same path. All these details should both be written in a letter kept with the actual regalia and books, and in your will, preferably drawn up by a solicitor. Legal people are not likely to be shocked or surprised if you want to ensure that your magical paraphernalia is

*Pagan Funeral Trust, BM Box 9290, London WC1N 3XX.

hood which celebrates communions or seasonal festivals for a congregation and the design of a satisfying funeral or memorial rite are all subjects which new pagans will need to explore. It isn't necessary to introduce a new orthodoxy, but rather design loose frameworks which will help anyone facing these crucial situations in their lives. It is important that thought and meditation is given fully to each stage of religious life. Birth and naming a child are important to its future development. Look at the way 'primitive' people name their children, giving a 'nick-name' at birth like Tiny or Rusty, until that individual grows up enough to show his or her characteristics, when a proper name is given. There may need to be the reintroduction of rites at puberty, to celebrate the new adulthood of the youngster, and later initiation rites to admit them into the magical life of the community. None of this should be rushed or done unthinkingly.

You need to plan for your death too, not only in the matter of preparing a will, or at least a letter stating your wishes, and the names of people to contact. That is urgent! You should spend time meditating on the process of death and dying. Learn how to sense the withdrawal of your spirit so that, should you become seriously ill, you can choose to withdraw and die, rather than linger in limbo, kept alive by medical science rather than a desire to live. Befriend death. See it as a great change. J. M. Barrie, Peter Pan's creator, wrote 'Death is a great adventure,' and so it is.

Initiation is a kind of trial death, for in the old days the candidate would be shut in a tomb, or buried in a sealed vault for several days and nights until he had a revelation, or the Goddess of Rebirth appeared to him and led him back to the light. If you study the books of published initiation rituals, you will often find fragments of this Death and Rebirth theme being retained. Today it is only a few minutes between the ritual binding and laying in the tomb or circle, and the rising up, reborn as an initiate, too swift, perhaps to gain the full force of the experience. Sadly, knowing what will happen in an initiation rite can diminish the effect because instead of being very aware of what is happening to you, on all kinds of levels of appreciation, you are waiting for the next phase, the familiar words or gestures, and anticipation can take away the impact of the event in that moment. Secret rituals are important for they do preserve the Mystery. Even a solo initiation, can, however, produce surprises, for the Gods will take a hand, and all manner of strange things can happen, no matter how well you think you are prepared. Don't rush to accept the first offer of initiation, just because it is quick. You are genuinely being 'reborn' and you need to think long and hard as to the kind of company which is going to accept you. The best option will catch up with you when you are really ready for it, have no doubt.

Throughout your life you will be able to follow an ever-growing and changing spiritual quest. Parts of it will be pursued alone, parts in the company of dear friends and co-workers. All the time you will be growing through spiritual dimensions, gaining insight and wisdom which will affect all the other aspects of your life. You will have to look at all the various religious and spiritual paths open to you. Read the literature and make up your own mind about the nature of the Cosmic Creator, Gods, Goddesses, the Holy Guardian Angel who may dwell within you, the anima or animus of your twin soul, elementals, beings from other worlds whether from other planets or stars, or from some great within, different realms of creation to our own. You will hear of Atlantean Adepts still sending their messages through the aeons of time, and visitors in flying saucers who have brought their own revelations to implant them in the minds of suitable messengers on Earth. You will need to look anew at the words of the great prophets and philosophers of old, the Gospels, the Koran, the Talmud, the writings of the Gnostics and the Dead Sea Scrolls. Reject nothing, no matter how weird it might be, for revelation comes in many forms, and though the messenger may seem outlandish, that which is revealed may be absolutely true, for you, and the kind of spiritual guidance you require.

You may come across all sorts of terms which are used in the language of spiritual revelation. You may hear of channelling, and of contacts and of Inner Plane Adepti, spacemen and Atlanteans, each passing on their teaching and instructions for a magical group, a school of initiates, or the world at large. In time, for it is one of the highest functions of the trained magician, you might learn how to 'channel' these ephemeral instructions for yourself. In one of Dion Fortune's novels, she has her hero, Dr Taverner (who was based on a real adept she worked with), switching himself into a channel so that 'lodge could talk to lodge' through both time and distance. This work is still carried on by individuals who are trained to become clear paths for the information which they are receiving for the benefit and instruction of their own people. Some perform this service in a fully aware state within the working of a lodge, relaying messages and guidance to those around them; others write automatically, producing teaching material or whole books by direct inspiration from some spiritual source. This is a very different activity to that of the spirit medium, who becomes a totally unconscious 'receiver' of non-material information. Magicians frown upon any state whereby you relinquish control over your body, mind or spirit, and though the kind of 'mediation' they do to receive cosmic information might seem to be the same, the 'mediator' is fully in control of his situation, he is totally protected by the enclosing circle of the lodge, and spiritually guarded by the Archangels invoked to his aid at the outset of the process.

The whole concept of religion is changing. The churches are looking hard at the ordination of women, the acceptance or rejection of homosexuals within the ministry, and some are changing their forms of service and language to keep up with modern trends to an extent that they have lost their original contact with the pure message of spiritual truth. Pagan, wiccan and non-orthodox churches are springing up, particularly in America, and are receiving recognition in terms of their legal status, and the validity of their teaching, marriages and baptism, etc. In other places the Celtic form of Christianity is being revived, as is Gnosticism. The ghosts of long-dead Cathars seem to be relaying their teachings to their reincarnated selves, and much ancient wisdom, religious guidance and spiritual power is being rediscovered from almost all the ancient pantheons and pagan teachings. If you are coming fresh to these ideas, be willing to look at different approaches to religion for the New Age, test and meditate on the inner meaning, the form of revelation, the spiritual needs of the community around you, and see which sacred path leads to the Temple of the Heart in your own life.

CHAPTER FIVE

The Royal Road to the Unconscious

Each night we dream but we dream unaware. If we do become aware
of a dream, it may be only as a passive bystander watching events
take place. Rarely do we discuss remembered versions of a dream
with a friend ... We do not usually consider the third of our life spent
asleep as an opportunity for self-discovery ... We have no psychological or cultural mechanism for allowing the dream consciousness to
enrich the remainder of life.

Robert E. Ornstein, THE PSYCHOLOGY OF CONSCIOUSNESS

The most important skills which will make an individual into a
successful magician are those of mind and consciousness. This is a
matter seldom discussed at length in any book on practical magic.
On the whole, such books concentrate on the equipment, the
regalia, the symbolism and the ceremonial acts, overlooking the
main reason why these external objects help to bring about the
purpose of the working. What all these different physical things
do is to focus that inner level of the mind specifically on the aim in
hand. For example, if you were working with the planet Jupiter,
in some problem concerning material finances, the books would
instruct you to perform your ritual on Thursday, wearing a robe

of blue, by an altar with four blue candles, and to create a talisman made of tin, whilst burning cedarwood incense, and so on. No one explains that all these 'corresponding' colours, numbers, symbols and special things relating to Jupiter work on your own inner levels of consciousness, acting like a lens to focus your intention upon Jupiterian matters.

These correspondences are really a set of elaborate stage props, but they are important and valuable, at least during any magician's training, because unless you can interact with the real objects you have little chance of being able to work with their magical counterparts. You have to learn to move and kneel in robes, to light charcoal and incense, to handle swords and cups, building up an indelible concept of these actions in your inner repertoire, so that, in your senior years as an adept, you can recall exactly the texture of the cloth, the smell of the incense, the weight of the goblet, for it is on this inner level that they are totally real. It is on the inner levels that the seeds sown in the outer ritual begin their growth. If the physical setting is correctly laid out it becomes a fertile seedbed for the new idea, help or healing which is the intention of the working. To act carelessly, or without due thought and attention leaves your magical intent's seed in an untended, stony and infertile growing medium, instead of fine tilth, warm and lifegiving.

It may seem strange, trying to train unapproachable levels of your mind by a form of careful playacting, but it is a tradition which is extremely ancient, and which continues, even at the very end of the twentieth century, because it is the best. Certainly those with many years of experience in the physical aspects of ceremonial magic do not need to get out their robes and regalia, their weapons and symbols for every piece of magical work they do, because deeply ingrained into their subconscious minds are all these practical skills, ready to be reawakened mentally at any moment. But many ritual magicians will prepare themselves and their temples, with full regalia and incense because they still enjoy the theatrical effects, and find they produce power and assist in the working. The power resides in the mind of the magician, however, not in the instruments, symbols or regalia. Certainly all those things which are dedicated to use in magical work do change in their nature when they are consecrated, but the power is always inherent in the magician, not his equipment. This can be demonstrated by anyone who might be shown the instruments and regalia of magic by an experienced practitioner. They might be allowed to hold his pentacle or cup but they will not acquire his power or control over magical forces during the loan of the charged items. Only prolonged dedication can bring the necessary focus and control of the forces which are the essence of effective magic.

Every one of us has inner abilities, powers of creativity and healing, or personal resource and strength, and most of the complex training of an adept is aimed towards opening those secret doors to our individual, inner awareness. Meditation, creative visualisation and pathworking, though they may at first seem dull, are crucial to developing an understanding, and then a control of these essential skills, which have no obvious physical counterpart. Because they are subtle and ephemeral and cannot be perceived and measured in the way that muscular strengths or physical prowess can be, the standard which any individual has reached is largely subjective. You cannot prove that you have become a 'Grade 3 Meditator' or a 'First-Class Visualiser' to the outside world. Certainly a well-trained magician could deduce this by examining any candidate, both with questions and by scanning him psychically, but on the whole, solo students, or those working with friends, have to become their own judges as to how much progress they have made at any of these mental and spiritual practices.

Freud was one of the first people in modern times to pay any heed to dreams. In his forms of analysis he discovered that the symbols and ideas, the exploits and adventures, which patients recalled and related to him during psychoanalysis gave the dimmest glimmer of what was going on in their troubled minds. In his particular interpretation he found mainly sexual problems, which seems, in the light of re-examination, to have said more about his own life than about that of his patients. However, he did set out a path towards the subconscious, the buried levels of everyone's mind which could be examined by others, who could then offer guidance and advice. Carl Jung, who recognised in his patients the inherent desire for religious experience, as well as the most basic animal drives, took this path further, expanding his study of dreams into the realms of mythology and legend. These ancient stories gave him an understanding of 'archetypes', specific sorts of characters who turn up, time and again, in legends and folk-tales. The ever-conquering Hero, the Old Wise Woman, the Mother, the Shadow hidden within each individual, the Child and the Joker, each of whom, to a greater or lesser degree, can be perceived in most people, if their characteristics are examined closely.

Jung was wise enough to realise that what a symbol or character meant to one person could be different for another, and tried to get his patients to look at each, as they turned up in dreams or waking visions, to discover what they meant to the individual concerned. This is an aspect of his work which must be taken seriously by every modern student of magic. We have to learn to perceive our dreams clearly, remember them, record them, and analyse them, for in them may lie the keys to the future, the pattern of the way we will go forward, the outcome of our magical acts. We all have a free access to this form of information but, like all magical skills, it takes time to come to grips with our nocturnal adventures, our sleeping exploits and those activities which appear so real and yet are only occurring within our uncontrolled subconscious minds.

One of the oldest aspects of magic, frequently recorded in ancient Egypt, in the Bible and in other old sources, is the recounting and interpretation of dreams, particularly those of the king or ruler. This antique form of divination was seen as an uncluttered way of gaining information from the Gods or angels, and even if the symbols seen were obscure, or the message complicated, someone, either a Seer or Prophet, or even the dreamer, properly instructed, could understand what was being implied. The same idea holds true today. You have to become aware of the sort of dream you have each night, its content and implications, and only by making the effort to record all that you remember every night for at least six months can you hope to build up enough data to start to analyse the symbols, the images and the events in your personal dream-time. You have to ac-knowledge, at least to yourself, your fears and failings, your needs and objectives, which may each be clearly reflected in your sleeping visions. Only you can judge and value and weigh up the material which is given to you, direct from the unconscious regions of your mind. It is no simple task, but by regularly examining the content, form and nature of your dreams you will begin to see patterns emerging. Some of these will be a true reflection of the tides of psychic awareness which the Moon casts upon your sleep. Like all animals and plants, every individual is affected to a small extent by the Moon's phases, and gradually by noting the vividness or variety of your dreams will you come to see how her shifting and gentle light is acting upon your sleeping mind. You may not necessarily sleep with your curtains drawn back so that the full moon can shine upon your bed, but the subtle, inner influences of the moon's beams will in some way influence how and what you dream.

You will have to note down how you dream: in full colour or in black and white; if you are involved in the action or present but merely a witness to it, or if you remain detached, an observer, like someone watching television. You will have to discover if all dreams are the same; narrative adventures, symbolic images or strange unformed shapes which are hard to pin down. You will have to see how the power and clarity of your dreams waxes and wanes through the lunar cycle. Are they brighter at the full moon and dim at the new? You alone will have to look for the pattern, individual to you. You will have to explore any symbols or landscapes in meditation, focusing your whole attention on uncovering what the import of each night's events might be. Are your dreams simply entertainment? Are they data processing? Are they predictive or do they bring you new sources of wisdom and deeper understanding of your unique nature?

You can make this sometimes difficult process easier by being aware how many hours of sleep you need. Go to bed a little earlier so that you can allow nature to wake you rather than the strident tones of an alarm clock, the certain destroyer of dream memory. Try to spend a few moments in silent contemplation of what you can recall on waking, jot down notes and rely on a few moments going over these during quiet times in the day. Gradually you will discover that your memory improves, both for dreams and ordinary matters from the waking hours. By recollecting aspects of each night's dream you shift them from the ephemeral parts of your short-term memory into the more enduring regions of long-term memory. It is the same process as is used when remembering phone numbers, etc. Repeat them over a few times and you can recall them later, simply look them up in the book and don't repeat them, and if you don't get through, you have to look them up again. Try it!

Everyone dreams. Many men think they don't but this is just because they have never bothered to teach themselves to recall this seemingly useless material each morning. It also seems to be a right-brain function to remember dreams, and many men, in particular, seem to live so much of their waking hours with the left-logical-brain thinking being dominant that it is quite an effort to make use of the more intuitive right brain. Those who work creatively, male or female, have far less difficulty with any of the mental skills of practical magic. To them the process of path-working, meditation, and dream recall are all parts of everyday life and so these intangible arts come more easily to them. Like all the processes of magic, the more you do each one the easier it gets.

Dreams offer an unrecognised channel of information direct from the deepest levels of our inner minds. They are not censored or limited by the events of real life. In dreams we can fly, travel to other worlds, we can grow as big as a planet, shrink to micro-scopic size, live in the past or the future, on this plane or any other. We can seem to go even beyond our wildest, conscious, dreams! First we must learn to explore, record and analyse, then, eventually we can begin to control and shape where we go, bodiless, at night.

Many of the traditional arts of magic, or rather, those attri-buted to magicians by fiction writers, include astral travel, time travel and other mysterious sounding arts. Each of these is a viable proposition but each, in turn, requires absolute control over the subconscious mind, just as does effective meditation and creative visualisation. All these skills are related to each other, so the better you become at any one of them, the easier the others get. There aren't any short-cuts though, and no potion, no magic wand, no initiation can grant you the ability to make use of these inwardly directed senses except continued and serious practice. They all require a certain knack, and, like the ability to swim or ride a bicycle, you find you can suddenly do it. Water-divining is just the same. There is no intermediate stage – either you can or you can't! Most of these mental skills can best be learned in a light-hearted way, too, rather than the deadly serious, teeth-gritted stance which some would-be meditators adopt. You can try too hard, and lose the subtle, relaxed attitude which makes it possible to gently open the inner doors to your unknown mind, and more important, to close them firmly when you have completed a particular exercise.

Astral travel is a technique by which your entire consciousness is projected outside your resting body, to explore other times and places. It is a difficult skill to master, and can be dangerous if you are disturbed while you are actually 'out-of-your-body', for it can give you a nasty shock. There are plenty of modern books which give a variety of techniques for mastering this particular activity, so if you want to have a go, read these, and follow the instructions carefully. Some of you may find a technique by which you imagine yourself standing in front of you, and then project your awareness into it, will work; whilst others prefer to sort of 'roll out' of their bodies, whilst lying in bed, before sleep. What is hardest is to retain an awareness of what you are doing and where you are trying to go. It is always much easier in works of fiction, like most magical arts, than it is in real life!

A slightly simpler, and infinitely more useful skill is that of projection of consciousness, rather than your astral self. In this you remain in a relaxed and aware state whilst sending some level of your attention off on a journey through time and space. In this state, really a form of deep meditation, you can talk and explain to a companion, what you are seeing or experiencing. Like all these techniques it does take a fair bit of practice, and it does need the assistance of a reliable and totally trustworthy companion, who will ask questions and take notes as you seem to float through the aether. It is no good getting to some interesting otherwhere or otherwhen at the moment your friend has gone to make a cup of tea! It is a way of discovering aspects of your own previous lives, if you so wish, for by directing your own attention to another landscape, or by having your companion lead you there on a suitable pathworking journey, you can become your previous self, reliving aspects of that lifetime in full – and sometimes gory – detail. Be prepared!

In any activity when you are not going to be one hundred per cent aware of your immediate surroundings, whether it be a simple, brief time of meditation, or the prolonged and distracted mentation of projection through time or space, you should make proper preparations first. It is important always to approach these sessions with a degree of anticipation and yet not become too excited as to what you might learn or experience. During your explorations you should aim to be both physically relaxed and calm, whilst being mentally alert and attentive to what you hope to discover. You will need to make some obvious preparations, like telling your household you won't be available for half an hour, and that you need relative peace and quiet. It helps to provide yourself with a biscuit and fruit drink, even a thermos flask of hot tea or coffee, if you are likely to make a prolonged journey through the astral planes, as you can get very cold. Ensure that your companions are aware of what you are trying to do, with precise instructions about silence or asking questions, recording your words on tape or writing them down (preferably both, as magical atmospheres can upset the most robust of electronic equipment!) Teach yourself to be able to adopt a comfortable but supported physical position, while remaining both still and relaxed. It does matter that you can breathe easily, and are not cutting off your circulation to your head or feet by permitting your neck to slump or having your legs crossed. These unbalanced positions have adverse esoteric effects as well, so do aim for balance, stillness and comfort before you begin. These factors also tend to enhance the material you receive, or the depths of the experience.

In magical work the idea of trance states is not one to be encouraged. In American books the word 'trance' is used in a slightly different way to the way it is commonly used in British magical literature. What is meant, I believe, in both places, is a state of relaxed mental detachment, where none the less, the individual is still in total control, being able to observe what is happening inside his head, and being able to terminate the experience fully and quickly for whatever reasons make this necessary. The most useful and effective states are those which are fully induced, controlled and ended by the conscious will of the individual undergoing them. There are a few occasions where an experienced magician might lead a group or individual along a path through the levels of awareness to a deeper state than these people are normally able to achieve on their own, but this is only done within a school or lodge, for a specific purpose. You need to learn to be able to switch quickly to the correct level for whatever sort of work you are doing, be it meditation, time travel or ritual working, and to be able to switch back to ordinary awareness quickly, safely and under full control. Again, there is no easy way except continuous practice.

Some people enter the altered states of consciousness by feeling warm and light, others feel cool and heavy. Some experience a floating and detached sensation, others an earthy deepness, as if sinking down into the very ground below. Some have precise and clear impressions of all the images, places, faces, times and experiences, others have only shadowy recollections of dim shapes and colours. What you perceive will depend on your own psychic make-up, but like any other skill, the more you can work on it the easier and more controlled it becomes. Note down your own experiences so that by mentally replicating these, imagining how you feel rather than what you should be seeing, you will find you get through the veils of consciousness gently and effectively.

Try listening to a variety of kinds of quiet music and seeing what changes these bring about in your awareness. See what different scents from flowers, vaporising oils or incenses do to you. Experiment with positions, clothing, warmth and so on to discover the optimum conditions which lead you towards those doors to inner awareness. Record any attempt, with as much detail as you can, for you may well be able to help others in the time to come. What helps you may well help companions with whom you share later experiences.

Get into the habit of looking at your state of awareness, even during the day, in quiet moments. Learn to observe how you feel as you drift off to sleep, or when you are day-dreaming, or nodding off in front of the television. Look at the world around you. Notice the seasonal changes in parks and gardens as well as the countryside. Watch the way the moon's shape changes during her cycle, see also how where she rises and sets vary along the horizon, as opposed to the sun's regular progress through the year, rising and setting east and west only at the equinoxes. Observe when and how the trees come into leaf and when the golden brown of autumn gilds the branches and landscape, and when the leaves actually fall in your part of the world. These things may seem unimportant, and in no way related to your own changing state of awareness, but you will come to discover, when you start to use any form of divination, that you may see scenes, or be aware of seasonal changes as the only clues about the time events may come to pass. If you can't tell when the trees are in leaf, or when they shed their covering you will be unable to predict accurately. Also, the changing year will affect your inner processes, and you too will seem to grow and blossom, and then sink back and rest, in regular cycles, but you must watch out for these to judge them for yourself.

Observation is a hard thing to learn as an adult. If you were always curious as a child you will automatically inspect the world around you for unspoken clues which are so valuable in divination, particularly the old art of scrying. In this method, when you relax into your level of inner awareness and then concentrate your gaze within the speculum, the crystal ball, the black mirror or a bowl of water, you will begin to see symbols, shapes, colours and perhaps, eventually, scenes and events from the future. It is this particular skill which needs both the controlled ability to relax and to see, and the trained memory to recognise what you are seeing and interpret it. Scrying is one of the hardest of all the magical skills, for unlike ritual or symbolism it isn't a matter of conscious learning and practising, but rather an ability to relax alertly and switch on a different level of perception. No one can predict in advance what sort of images you might see, and like dreams, what you see is largely subjective and varies from individual to individual far more than most things in magic. Unlike meditation or creative visualisation there is no obvious starting-point or framework to guide what you perceive. You are on your own, trying to relax enough to see clearly, yet remain alert enough to take note and intepret what the vision offers. Again, it is the power within you to alter the focus to some other level of reality, not a magical virtue within the crystal ball or other speculum. Many people do find, at least at first, that a dark glass is easier to see in than a shiny ball or bowl of clear water.

The most effective way to achieve results at scrying is to meditate first for a few minutes, allowing that change into an altered state to creep over you, before you turn to the speculum. Make sure that the lights are fairly dim and that there is no point of brightness which will reflect within the speculum and distract you. Make sure, too, that the table on which the dark glass rests is not too low, or you will end up crouching over it like an old dame hunched over her cauldron. This isn't very good for your breathing, and so inhibits your ability to see and remember. Focus your sight within rather than on the surface of the glass or water and sink within it. Traditionally the vision tends to become misty or smoky to begin with, and then a patch of a darker colour starts to form. This may seem to be a swirl or hole through which other images gradually come into focus. Some people see as clearly as watching a film; others see only shapes, colours, symbols or letters of the alphabet, so it is not as simple a process as looking at the Tarot cards, for example. You have to do all the work. The more detached you can become, the clearer the pictures form, but you do have to interpret and understand these, especially if you are attempting to read the future for some other person. They will expect you to predict time, place, people and events, whereas you might see vague landscapes, misty images, blurred letters! It certainly is an art which requires even more attention than any of the symbolic systems of divination, like the Tarot, the I Ching or the Runes. These at least come with a book of instructions, whereas, like dream images, those things seen in a glass, darkly, do not.

When you wish to explore other times or places you will need to prepare as well. The first thing to recognise is that once you slip into an unscripted journey you cannot so easily predict how long it might take, nor how far you are able to go. It is, of course, much better if you are able to make your preliminary voyages through other realms in the care of an experienced traveller. This is a twofold protection because anyone new to such journeys, and adventuring for the first time is likely to be extremely enthusiastic, especially if, through doing plenty of meditation exercises first, they are able to arrive at the most effective state of mind quickly. The unwary novice traveller may well try to prolong the experiment, staying 'out' for more than about half an hour, and this is a strain on the psyche, whereas the expert will help him return as soon as there is any sign of difficulty. The second hazard is trying to remember all that has been perceived. Again, an expert can ask appropriate questions, and guide the traveller through the unfamiliar process, so that he gets the most out of his early, hesitant travels. When another novice is trying to guide a friend through the strange and seemingly endless mind-scapes it really is a case of the blind leading the blind. Inner journeys through the known world are always safest. A simple trip to a friend's house, 'on the astral', as it were, might surprise the friend, if he is psychic (for he might just sense your invisible presence as a sort of ghost), and it might surprise you, to discover what is going on at a distance, but it is the best road to tread while you are learning. Look at a clock, if there is one, and note the time. See if there is a newspaper or TV programme which would help identify the date. It might seem logical that you would be seeing the other place simultaneously as you are resting somewhere else, but this is not always the case!

Try to see some piece of furniture or tabletop where certain objects will be placed and changed from time to time. If you see any people, observe what they are doing. It does take practice to actually see and hear what is going on at a distance from your body with any degree of accuracy, for the conscious mind has a habit of interfering, imposing a scenario, dialogue and action on what you perceive at a distance, so you cannot be sure, to begin with, if what you see has been made up or is true. Again, you will need to keep records and check up! Be a bit tactful too, for it is all very well visiting a friend in the daytime, but if they catch on with what you are doing and you start to make night-time trips there could be embarrassment, not to say hostility, at your uninvited visitation, real or imaginary, so behave with responsibility. It

may seem like fun to visit a girlfriend's home at night to see what
she is up to, but is it fair on her? Is it going to enhance your
relationship in the long run? How would you like to be spied on?
Think it over before you do anything you could be sorry for later.

Responsibility is an important concept in magic. You do need
to be aware of what you are doing and its possible consequences,
at all times. There is no excuse, nor can you pitifully say, 'I didn't
believe it would work,' because unless you have some suspicion
that any magical act or experiment will work there is no point
doing it in the first place. You must always act as if your spell or
ritual or talisman *will work*, and soon. You must try to envisage
any consequences, both for yourself and anyone else who is
involved. Look at the long-term as well as the short-term effects
of a healing, for example, or the desire for the solution to a
personal relationship problem. To work a spell for eternal love
might lead to just that, on the day that you meet another person
who takes your heart! Magic has a quirky way of coming about,
and there is many a disappointed novice who has had his dream
come true, only to find that he had by then changed his mind to
some other objective, which is then put beyond his reach, by the
Laws of Magic!

Bear these factors well in mind, because you are always
responsible for the outcome of any occult work you do, for good
or ill. You may *mean no harm* but if in the end result someone is
harmed, it is your fault, and by the Law of Threefold Return you
will suffer the consequences. Some of the results will come home
to you, for if you dash into mental or psychic activities before
you are really ready for them you can reasonably expect some
sort of side-effect. If you rush out on astral journeys, unprepared
and without guidance or the application of common sense, the
chances are you will be in for some disturbing experiences. You
will affect your sleeping pattern, and quite often nightmares,
which are really the residue of unabsorbed psychic experiences,
will come to haunt your nights. You may feel you are 'under
psychic attack', and so you are, but only from your own inner
dustbin of unexamined material which has been cast up by your
careless poking about.

Some students of the occult, who have been led on by books of
easy spells, or Instant Enlightenment, find there seems to be a
presence lurking around them, some dark shadow which is
perceived at the edge of vision, by day and night. They are certain
that their fumbling attempts at magic have awoken the wrath of a

real Black Magician who has sent 'a nasty' to get them. What is really troubling them is their own Shadow, quite literally. For the first time the subtle levels of ordinary awareness have been expanded to bring into focus the darker side of the student's own nature. It has always been there, it is just that any kind of psychic activity, be it basic meditation, simple pathworking and the like, will have expanded perception just enough for it to appear around the edge of the screen of reality. It cannot be banished, and many novices do try really hard to apply all sorts of high-powered banishing rituals to this aspect of their own beings. Instead of fading quietly into the mist, as the books would suggest, this Shadow gets bigger and blacker, and more haunting. The way to deal with it is by acknowledging its existence, as part of yourself. It may be the forgotten self, the ignored self, the repressed self, even, but it is still a real, and actually valuable, part of the complex and unique being which is you. Get to know it, befriend it and it will guide you safely through the realms in which it is more at home. Become aware of the failings and faults you have, and try, in the light of that knowledge, to cope with them and overcome them. Look at the past, meditate on it, alone and secretly, until you banish the dark shadow and it becomes a shining light, ready to illumine the path before you. Learn to accept the guidance of this evolving aspect of your being, permitting it to know your doubts and fears, and find ways of working in harmony so that you can overcome them. It is a part of the landscape of the mind, and will be far more use if you allow it to function properly, as your conscience or Guardian Angel.

This Guardian may well also turn up in dreams, to protect you from real dangers, like straying too far from the path of reason on your early journeys through that realm. You may begin to see it as a beautiful woman, or handsome man, accompanying you on your inner travels. It may take the form of a great totem animal, or a small familiar, for being of shadow-substance, it can shape-shift at will, or if you request it to change, perhaps it will obey, becoming a knight in shining armour, or a wizard, or a heroine, ready to help. That choice is yours, but if out of fear or lack of knowledge you try to drive it away, it will seem to grow larger, and really haunt your dreams.

You have to look carefully at anything symbolised, whether in dream or meditation or during day-dreams. It is only by referring to your own memories, understanding of mythology, studies of the vast literature on esoteric and legendary topics that anything you perceive in these inner-mind states will have any real meaning. What you discover will be, to a large extent, individual and subjective. Books on dream interpretation may give only the haziest help, for they are compiled from earlier sources, often part whimsical Victorian notions, part misinterpreted Freud, part total imagination. In modern terms it is best that you take any significant symbol and meditate on it, asking all the while for it to be made clear to you.

An example might be if someone dreamed of a box. To one person it could represent a gift – simple enough. To another it could mean 'present', and then rather than meaning a gift it could imply that attention needed to be paid to living in the 'present' time rather than the past. Another dreamer seeing a box might interpret it as a cage which shuts him in, while someone else, suffering from a lack of security, might see the box as a safe haven into which she can escape the problems of the world. Almost any object can be seen and considered in many ways, and it is your own feelings, at the time of the dream or vision, the state of your perceived world, the things which are troubling or pleasing you which add weight to the meaning of any dream picture.

Interpretation becomes more complex when you venture into the realms of divination, for even with the clear symbolism of the Tarot cards, for example, you have to discover what any image might imply to the person for whom you are doing the reading. Something which to you would mean a pleasant surprise could offer a frightening threat to another person. You must be well aware that all forms of divination are dealing with the concept of change, for it is that factor which makes each of us evolve through our chains of interlinked lives. The many magical arts are really concerned with recognising the omens of impending change, whether these be seen in dream, vision, meditation or through divination, and then being ready to cope with the change as it comes, either by bending like the reed, and allowing change to shake but not disturb you, or by actively flowing with it, to make the best use of the energy of the flooding tide. The symbols you see may well indicate whether the change will be gradual or sudden, a great alteration to the world as you know it, or a gentle growing into a new era.

Only by getting to know the images presented by your subconscious mind, the way they eventually work out in real life, can you really take full control of your life and future. Through knowing how things change in your own life you will be able, to some degree, to predict changes in the lives of those whom you wish to help or who ask you for advice. It is not a simple task, nor can it be quickly achieved. You have to plug away at it, over the months and years, gradually building up data, becoming aware of your impressions, feelings, and intuitions about anything you discover whilst voyaging under control through the inner worlds, or whilst gliding through them in the free-fall of dreams.

CHAPTER SIX

The Crossroads of Tradition

If you came this way,
Taking any route, starting from anywhere,
At any time, or at any season,
It would always be the same:
You would have to put off
Sense and notion. You are not here to verify,
Instruct yourself or inform curiosity
Or carry report. You are here to kneel
Where prayer has been valid ...
Here, the intersection of the timeless moment
Is England and nowhere. Never and always.

T. S. Eliot, LITTLE GIDDING

Looking at the magical world from the outside, the average
student has no concept of how many varying paths there are
within the labyrinth of the Western Tradition. He may well have
come across references to witchcraft, for this has had a great deal
of publicity, mostly sensational, in the last couple of decades.
From reading he will have come across mentions of the Hermetic
Tradition, the Golden Dawn, Freemasonry and the Qabalah, but

few of these are discussed in a context which shows them to be paths which an individual might follow, or societies he might join.

Magical groups of all traditions have always been cloaked in secrecy. They do not seek publicity or converts; nor on the whole do they appear in any easily approachable setting, so that Seekers can openly explore the wisdom they offer, ask questions of the Brethren, or discuss their aims and objectives. It is a daunting task for the novice who is a sincere and dedicated student to find any group which will offer training, or, better still, initiation. Certainly, in the back of some of the readily available astrological and occult magazines on sale in newsagents, there are small advertisements for various groups or covens or societies, and for some, this may well provide an adequate first step. It is in this part of the maze that the clues are vaguest, the path most convoluted, the dead ends most frequent.

One of the main reasons harks back to the concept of secrecy. Each valid and effective group, be it a Society, Fellowship or Order will be made up of quite a small number of initiates, frequently only about ten in number, which grows by only one or two members each year. Even if there were many hundreds of such groups in the country, the annual intake would still be very small, and it is not recorded anywhere just how many groups there actually are. To find a suitable group and to be accepted by them, be it a coven of witches or a lodge of high or ceremonial magicians is a great honour. That fact is seldom appreciated by those who imagine that to join such an élite order is as simple and convenient as signing up for evening classes at the local Adult Education Centre. It really is hard to find any kind of valid group which will offer safe and beneficial training to all those who request it.

Another reason which makes it so hard for an outsider to become an insider is that the novice outsider has no real appreciation of what goes on within the various sorts of groups, and so may not be able to decide if he or she wishes most to become a witch or a ceremonial magician. Certainly, there are far more covens advertising for new members than there ever were lodges of ritual magicians seeking trainees, but the beginner may find it hard to ensure he is making the right decision, especially if he acknowledges that any initiation is for real and cannot be rescinded if he changes his mind once he is in. Also, quite often, those covens which are advertising for new members have split off from others and may contain those members who quarrelled with the parent coven, and whose High Priestess and High Priest may not yet have the knowledge and experience to make them magically effective. Groups which divide amicably usually do so because they already have more than enough initiated members, be they covens or lodges, and so are not in the market to take in a large number of would-be insiders.

Magical groups are powerful entities. If they are made up of fully trained magicians or witches they will have a potent effect upon the psyches of any new members who are admitted to them. Certainly, within a well-established lodge or coven there is a terrific feeling of comradeship, love and respect for all members which has been developed, often over many years of hard and close-knit work together. Any new influence brought in by a newcomer will swiftly be overwhelmed and transformed by the group soul, or collective unconscious of the established group. Like many of the experiences in magical training, it may not be wholly enjoyable for the novice! Even if the group has the best possible motives in the world the effect its group soul will have on the newcomer may feel strange and unsettling. It is a frequent complaint of new initiates that they feel haunted or overlooked by some strange presence. Just as was explained in the previous chapter, deeper aspects of the individual are awoken by magical practices, and when these are enhanced by a powerful group soul, the effect can be very alarming indeed. It is not harmful, merely a clear demonstration that magical reality is real, and is a potent force within the world.

Any really effective group will be well aware of the effect its initiation may have on the novice, and will normally have put him through a long and intensive training before admitting him. This protects the unity of the group as well as being more gentle on the psyche of the new initiate. It shows that the novice has sufficient patience, persistence and dedication to pursue his studies before he is launched into the power and glory of full ritual. It also ensures that he has a thorough knowledge of the system, the symbolism, the mythology, god-forms and all the other matters which it is imperative that any working magician understands before beginning working with those unseen forces. To be simply thrown into a ceremony when you have no idea of the words you are to speak, the meaning of any gestures made, and any angelic or god-forms invoked does nothing for the power of the ritual and little for the benefit of the newcomer.

Magic in any form is a participation activity. It is not a spectator sport to be watched and simply viewed from outside. Each person within the circle or temple has a part to play, minor or major depending on their training and position. As images are described, all must try to visualise them; as journeys are followed, all must feel they are treading them together. When religious festivals are celebrated, all must share the worship, and when communions are partaken, each one must accept them wholeheartedly. It is this working in close harmony which multiplies the power which any effective group will have over the same number of individuals working alone or in a loose association. It is certainly possible for one or two trained magicians to raise a fair head of power on their own, but they will not be quite as effective as a really harmonious and close-knit group.

If you desire to belong to any sort of group you will have to make considerable efforts in two directions. The first is to learn the necessary, basic skills so that you have the perception to recognise the value of any training offered, or the intentions of any individual or group. This ensures that you have at least a comforting sense of kinship with them before getting further committed. Always go by your own feelings, no matter how good the opportunity seems, or how quickly admission to a group is offered. To rush into some set-up which doesn't really suit you, or when you have any misgivings, may lead to a situation you regret later on. The second path you must seek towards the heart of the Mystery Tradition will be found in the world around you. You must locate a group, lodge, coven or school, and the only clues you may have will appear in some public source of information.

In Britain alone there are over a hundred small magazines, journals and newsletters, many of which are produced by esoteric groups or schools. Many deal with witchcraft, paganism, occult philosophy, research into UFOs, parapsychology, the Qabalah, Eastern and Western traditions, divination, astrology and much more. To begin to discover these you will need to examine the small advertisements in the more readily available journals. Another literary source from which you might capture the thread leading to the group you most desire to meet will be found in books written by living authors. If you have enjoyed the work of any writer there is always the possibility that he or she may run a school or some form of instruction. Some writers lead weekend workshops, both in Britain and in Europe, or in the USA, or hold seminars to discuss and practise particular arts. All authors are pleased to hear from their readers, and comments are always read with interest. This is particularly true in the Western Mystery Tradition for much of the material being written about today is the result of research and experimentation, based on ancient knowledge, which is being reworked and expanded to suit modern students of the occult. You do need to be sure that the author is still likely to be alive, as many recently published occult books are in fact reprints, but a quick glance at the publishing history will tell you when the first edition of the book was issued. If it is within the last ten years then that author may well still be teaching in some way. Don't expect to be taken on as a solo student though, for most writers are very busy people, researching their next book, or travelling round the world giving instruction.

You might discover that monthly popular magazines have articles by witches or healers who, again, may be contacted through the magazine's offices, or through television stations who have documentary films, or chat shows. Local radio stations often have occasional broadcasts on magic, witchcraft, dreams, ghosts and so on, so an acute ear to the phone-ins might provide a first contact with someone who knows about various esoteric subjects. Of course, some of those who get into the media do so because they like the publicity, and enjoy showing film crews around their 'secret' magical temple, or performing rituals in front of the cameras, but you must use your own developing judgement. Some will have a genuine message, and will be happy to hear from Seekers, others are there for the show and their knowledge may be shallow.

Another public source of information which may be helpful to those who seek companionship along the path might be found in lectures, evening classes and organisations, like the Theosophical Society, which has branches in many towns, advertising their public meetings in the local library. If you enquire you will find that many different kinds of fellowships hold meetings in even the most improbable places! It is worth attending local ancient history talks and slide shows by the ecologists, or evening classes on various forms of alternative therapy, for though these may not, in themselves, be the subject you most desire to study, there is always a chance that other people will attend these gatherings who also seek knowledge of the Mysteries. Sometimes you will encounter well-established witches and magicians who are always trying to learn more about the world they live in, about the developments in old healing techniques and so on. Get to know your fellow students, drop discreet hints about your other interests and you may find someone will turn up who can help you himself, or can put you in touch with friends who can. Those arts which have always been secret are not easy to discover, but many of the people involved will recognise the sincerity of your aims, and because most magical folk are encouraged to give help and information if they are asked, you will find unexpected friendship there.

If you are able to decide which of the many paths you wish to follow then you can magically work to make contact with those who also tread that road. The more you learn about yourself, your dreams, occult aims and ambitions, and the better you get at the information-retrieving arts of meditation and creative visualisation, the closer you will come to gaining that important contact with the like-minded souls. Solo meditation may seem a far cry from joining in with others in seasonal festivals or ceremonial magic, but it can bring this objective into reality if you allow it. Meditation opens up those gates to inner perception, and it is that awareness which permits you to notice the announcement of a lecture, the advertisement for a society's open meeting or other gathering. In all probability, such adverts are frequently printed, but it is that new alertness which helps you to notice them when you are ready to take the next step. It is the latest version of the old adage, 'When the student is ready, then the teacher will appear!' That readiness is usually shown by your recognition of the importance of some very ordinary piece of information, which has always been available to you, suddenly taking on a new meaning.

It does help to have some basic idea as to which path you most wish to follow, and that will only come from a fair amount of reading or study. Do make use of your local library, for through the inter-library loan service they have access to all the books in English held in the British Library lending service. It might be a while before the book you want is available to you, but you can request it, so long as you know the title and publisher, the author and date of publication. Most libraries will help you trace these details. Another way to get hold of interesting magical or esoteric books is by getting your name on the lists of any of the second-hand book suppliers. There are at least a dozen whose lists consist entirely of occult works, both new and out-of-print. For a small fee, or even a stamped addressed envelope, in some cases, you can receive a regular list of their stock, and for half the price of the new title, you may be able to have an earlier issue sent to you. These lists are also very useful for reference, for they will give the details needed for applying for the books on loan. You might also live in a town which has a good selection of second-hand bookshops in it. These will often have older and rarer magical books hidden away on their shelves if you use your newly awoken psychic senses to look. You often find that during meditation or dreams a certain image representing a book title keeps flitting across your point of awareness, and on your next visit to the library or bookshop, there is a book which makes your dream come true.

The list of possible directions you might choose to take is enormous, varying from the ancient solo shamanistic ways to those of the Aquarian magician who is mastering the techniques which will take him into the next Age. You will have to decide how important mental arts are, how you feel in a religious sense, for all aspects of practical magic require an acknowledgement of God or at least a Cosmic Life Force from which our magical power is ultimately derived. You may wish to worship many gods and goddesses, or you may prefer to expand your healing abilities, your skills as a diviner, or all the grandeur and paraphernalia of the ceremonial magician. You might fancy a solo path, closer to that of the medieval hermit, living and working for the good of the world alone. You might desire to be initiated into a coven and eventually become a High Priestess or High Priest of Wicca. Throughout our history many different schools of magical philosophy and practice have surged through Europe, and ended up in the USA, each leaving a few scattered clues for those who come now to gather and reconstruct. There are no unbroken threads of ancient wisdom, purely descended to initiates living at the end of the twentieth century, but there are enough pieces of the magical jigsaws for those with patience, or those with similarly minded companions to rebuild the ancient temples, redevelop the old forms of ritual, and worship again the Gods that made the gods.

Each path will lead into a separate layer of the labyrinth of the Western Mysteries. Each could take you a lifetime to explore and experience, and for a novice it is far safer to try one path alone first, and not mix up the symbolism and god-forms of many traditions. Be patient and give any chosen tradition at least a year before you reject it. Each will teach you things of value and awaken areas within your total being which will profit you in your future studies, whatever path they may take. The greatest danger in magic is to dabble. To gain a little knowledge of any skill or art and use it before you fully understand it, or have control over it, as has been said before, can lead to great disturbances within your mental and spiritual levels. Treat each pantheon of gods, each pattern of symbols, as a different country. You wouldn't try to speak Greek in France, or expect to find conventional English food in Turkey, so don't expect the inner realms to be all the same. They may all appear to be ancient and far away from you, but they are definitely not the same.

There is no simple way of describing the many different aspects of the Western Mysteries. Some are well documented and easily approachable, even if their roots may be far away in time and space. Others are definitely more local, and yet more obscure for they have not left a clearly written record, or an on-going tradition to follow. The following listing is roughly historical, yet many different philosophies overlapped, many were imported and took root in lands other than their native birthplace. In many places there were several separate magical and religious strands being woven at the same time. The names and natures of gods and goddesses were sometimes shared through many of the lands which are finitely bounded as countries now. Some gods and goddesses seemed to be the same with different names, but this is not necessarily so. In some long-lived traditions a number of completely different pantheons of gods and goddesses flourished over thousands of years, yet we tend now to mix them all up, as if they were all part of the same family. These facts should be thoroughly understood, and care should always be taken when you are addressing any deity. To begin with, work at these one at a time, asking for clear images, functions and symbols to be shown to you for each god and goddess, for example, until you recognise them by their faces, their sacred animals or their traditionally associated weapons, etc. Ask them and they will show you, so long as you are serious in your request.

The oldest magical tradition which has left its mark on our landscapes has no name and no clear purpose. All over Europe the megalith-builders raised standing stones, dug ditches, and over many hundreds of years created 'burial mounds', 'chambered tombs', long, round, disc and bell barrows. They set up sun-orientated circles and ellipses of standing stones, they set

markers to show the erratic rising and setting points of the moon.
They carved dips in the horizon and piled up mounds of earth and
cairns of stones. With the use of sophisticated mathematics yet
simple stone tools, they changed the face of their lands beyond
recognition, and their vast and varied works are to be seen and
wondered at to this day, in their thousands, from Orkney to
North Africa, from Ireland (and perhaps America) to China. We
cannot know what they celebrated at these scattered sites, we
cannot exactly determine who they worshipped, nor to whom
these places were built as memorials, for the scattered bones are
silent, and the exquisitely carved stones have not yet revealed
their hidden messages to us, their heirs. Science will not be able to
answer the questions which these fascinating monuments pose,
perhaps as much as ten thousand years since their construction,
but magic might. If Seekers are willing to venture through time to
the age in which the great stones were being raised, and witness
the construction of ancient sacred sites, a lot could be learned.
The messages surely stored in the crystals of the great rocks can
reveal the information encoded there if we master the art of
mental time-travel and can return through the ages to learn from
the technologists in the Stone Age their purpose and power.

After the aeons of the megalith-builders came the many ages of
the Classical Gods, of Ancient Egypt, of Greece and finally of
Rome. Each has left us plenty of clues, but also plenty of
questions. The Egyptians carved records on stone, wrote them in
pictorial hieroglyphs on papyrus and painted them upon the
enduring walls of their deep-dug tombs. We know the faces of
their gods and goddesses, of the several pantheons which succeeded each other through the long dynastic years. We can
understand much of the inscriptions, painstakingly decoded in
the last century, but we can only experience their undying
wisdom by personal efforts in this day and age. By approaching
the Goddess Isis we may learn something of her magical power,
her healing arts, her moon-led wisdom, but first we must understand the context in which she was worshipped, come to know
her husband/brother Osiris, her son, Horus.

The gods of the Ancient Greeks and Romans are perhaps more
familiar to us, for they name some of the days of the week, or
cities, such as Athens, Athene's town. Many words of Latin or
Greek have become jargon in new technologies, giving us a small
link with these mighty pantheons. The Romans brought their
knowledge, their practical skills, their architecture and their

religion to much of England, and the roads they paved, the walls they constructed, and temples at sacred sites they dedicated are still there to be seen today. Greek scholarship left many written records, as well as sacred and magical sites in many parts of Europe which may be visited and explored by today's pilgrim. Both these Classical sources are readily available to us, in translation, and by personal exploration, if that is a path we might wish to follow. The Romans brought strange arts of divination to Britain, they built around older shrines, encompassing the gods and goddesses of the place for ever in stone, and recording the Roman names of the deities on dedication altars and memorial tablets. Again, if we adventure through time, especially when seated within one of these temples or places of healing, we can approach quite close to the spirit of the place, as it is now, as it was in earlier times, and perhaps sense its even more ancient roots, buried deep and safe beneath the Roman remains or Greek sanctuary.

At the same time as the Greeks and Romans were expanding their empires and influence across the eastern flanks of Europe, the Celtic people were expanding their power to the West. Of course the two came into conflict, and the Celtic spirit was driven underground, to re-emerge when the Romans went home. Spain, Portugal, France, the Low Countries, parts of Germany, England, Wales, part of Scotland and Ireland were all the homelands of the Celts. Not a cohesive nation but rather a loose confederation of related peoples, individualistic and tribal, owing allegiance first to the clan and its chief and then to the regional king or ruler, they were looked upon by their Roman neighbours as strange and fearsome. Britain was thought of as the end of the world, the place where the dead went, and a place to be avoided at all costs.

The Celtic people had strong religious ties with each other, and they were guided, healed, taught and their laws upheld by the Druids, a magical priesthood with ancient roots. As much of Britain was wooded in the ages before the Romans brought their early industrialisation to the land, settlements were founded at fords and on ridges, jutting above the tangled forest. Rivers were roads, as hacking paths through the trackless wilderness was much harder than travelling by water. The Druids, whose name is probably derived from 'Drus', the oak tree, did not build temples, but planted groves of sacred trees, often oaks, and within these living chapels in the green they preserved the knowledge of their tribes in poem and song. To them writing down sacred things was anathema, and their inherited wisdom took as long as twenty years to instil into the initiates.

Druids were known for their knowledge of astronomy and astrology, their healing ability with both herbs and more magical cures, for changing the weather, and they kept historical records of each tribe and its members' ancestry in lengthy narrative verses. They could raise storms and tell the future, and when their tribe was involved in a battle, they would sing spells against the opposing army, insulting their king and naming the secret names of their local gods. They acted as teachers for the young, and keepers of the laws, being both judges and, when necessary, executioners of the convicted murderers. They made ritual sacrifices and led the people in their acts of worship. They foretold the future, both of individuals and of tribes. Although members of the modern Druid Orders in Britain are usually seen in public wearing white robes, in their own age, Druids wore brightly coloured clothes, probably many coloured tartans. Kings wore as many as twelve colours and Druids were allowed up to ten colours whereas the lower ranks of soldiers, peasants and farmers wore only a few colours.

There are a number of Orders of Druids in Britain; some are magical in their orientation, others perform a ceremonial duty at the Welsh eistedfoddau, providing Bards in blue, and Vates, the teacher/poets in green, as well as Druid priests in white robes and headdresses. Their sword-bearer asks if there is peace in the four directions, and leads the audience in the Druid's prayer. As well as the Welsh Druids, and several groups based in England, there are Cornish Bards, and Breton, Scottish, Irish and Manx orders of Druids, who, each in their own ways, strive to maintain many of the poetic and ceremonial duties of their ancient forebears. Several of these orders send representatives to join in the annual celebration at Stonehenge, when this is permitted by the authorities.

Other students have been exploring the fields of Celtic magical knowledge, reconstructing various versions of their Tree Alphabet, for the ancient Celts could write, using either Ogham, strokes carved on the edge of a squared stone memorial, or a tally stick, or using letters named after the native trees, perhaps using individual leaves as letters, to send messages. There is a vast unwritten record surviving in folk-takes, in calendar customs, in place names and around sacred springs and wells, many of which originally had Celtic goddesses as guardians. In many cases these have been Christianised into saints. Neither the Celts at large, nor the Druids, personified their gods and goddesses in the same way that the Romans did. They did not carve statues, but worshipped at the base of ancient trees, or where a spring of fresh water rose from the rock, or on the pinnacle of high hills and mountains. Many of these places are attracting the attention of modern magicians who are seeking to re-establish their links with nature, and draw power, as did the priests of old, directly from the Earth herself, at sacred places. There were often oracular priestesses who dwelt in caves or close to magical pools of dark, peaty water. At certain times of the year they would be asked to answer particularly important questions, or offer healing, or give forth guidance of a sacred nature.

The Celtic year, beginning about the start of November, has become enshrined in the practices of modern witches, who have special ceremonies at Hallowe'en, the Celtic Samhain (Summer's end) and Beltane (the feast of the Sacred Fire) early in May. The Celts also celebrated in February and in August, peak times in the natural agricultural year, but modern celebrants have fixed the dates on the calendars, just as the Christian Church fixed all its feast days, except for Easter, which still moves with the moon's phases. The Celts reckoned time by nights, rather than days, and in modern English we still have the word 'fortnight' taken from the fourteen nights of the Celts.

The Roman invaders did their best to stamp out the Druids for as a priesthood they were respected by the ordinary tribal folk, and their power both mundane and magical upset the Roman Empire's plans. The Druids would not worship statues of living emperors, who were declared to be gods by themselves, nor would they bow before images of the Roman's gods, even if they held some of the traditional powers attributed to the Celts' own gods and goddesses. However, it is from Roman sources that we have records of the titles of some of the Celts' deities – towns were named after them. For example, the modern city of Bath was called Aquae Sulis, the waters of *Sul*, the Celts' name for the goddess of the only hot spring in Britain. Like many of the sacred names in the Celtic calendar, Sul is a title, not a familiar name, for it means 'eye' or 'orifice', for where the hot, red spring water gushes forth from the stone there is an entry to the Otherworld where the Goddess in the Inner Earth rules supreme, and at this still sacred place, her birth waters with their continually life-giving and healing properties, come to our world. Trace the name of any old town and you will often find it is sacred to a god or goddess whose description has given the place its name.

When the Romans left Britain as their empire was collapsing from within and being defeated from without there was a resurgence of Celtic culture, art and, probably, religion. It was the time when the historical King Arthur, a late Celtic tribal chief, living in a Britain partly shaped by Roman roads and expansive farming and mining activities, gathered his bands of knights around a table, or within a circular hall, or ring of standing stones to fight off the encroaching Saxons. It was a time of religious conflict, between the surviving Druidic practices and the incoming early Christian influences, which had already been established at Glastonbury, by the building of a simple wattle church at the foot of the Tor before AD 100. The invading Saxons also had their own pagan faith.

Around Glastonbury there are many legends rooted in the land. Its strange Tor, standing like a bent pyramid above the then marshy lowlands, surrounded by a distant circle of hills and the flat glitter of the sea. Here Joseph of Arimathea is supposed to have brought the Holy Grail, and when he came to land, planted his thornwood staff in the hillside. This miraculously grew, and its offspring are to be found in the town to this day. They flower about Yuletide as well as late in May with other, ordinary hawthorns. Around the area is a vast Zodiac of great figures, laid out in ancient times by paths and hedges and the meandering patterns of streams and rivers. Some points are marked with small barrows, quarries and iron Age hill-forts, others overlain with modern roads and railways. From the air all twelve signs can be seen in their traditional forms, lying just where the stars of each constellation would indicate.

Many people have discovered important aspects of the Western Quest for Initiation within the search for the Holy Grail. This sacred vessel has many forms, both ancient and modern, and may be perceived in many ways. The idea of the questing journey is essential to the process of self-awareness, and whether it leads through the world at large, or to the immanence of the great within, has to be discovered by the pilgrim or seeker. The Arthurian codes of chivalry, the overcoming of strange beasts, the convoluted journey through the Wild Forest to arrive at the Grail Castle, to encounter and defeat various challenges to body and spirit, all have a valid place in the modern search for magical identity. In the familiar stories of knights and their ladies, of battles with giants and dragons, the magic of the wizard, Merlin, the enchantments of Vivienne Le Fay, and Arthur's final journey by boat to the sacred Isle of Avalon for eternal rest and healing each represent stages in our individual quests for self-knowledge and magical abilities.

The early Christian tradition, far removed from the modern churchianity, retained within it the spirit of the Celtic Church, with its healing ministry, its acknowledgement of women priests, its acceptance of married priests and the passing of bishoprics from father to son, and its close links with older Druidic practices, who also worshipped a God, sacrificed on a tree, had been largely forgotten. However, recent books and studies have revealed something of this early church's forgotten appeal, overwhelmed by the might of the Roman Church in about 600 AD, and scholars and mystics are re-examining its ways and celebrations, and they may live again.

Another aspect of the Church which was looked upon as heresy is that of *Gnosis*, the religion which taught one-ness with God through personal experience. It taught the dualistic concept of God being totally spirit and never being made flesh in the person of Jesus, who was also pure spirit: and the Demiurge, the *Rex Mundi*, lord of all creation, who was not God. The Gnostics, the Cathars, the Albigensians all adhered, even to death by burning, to the principles of this twin deity. They did not see creation as evil, merely different from God. Their priests, male and female, were called *Parfaits*, the Perfected Ones, who had lived their lives on earth, brought up their families before dedicating themselves wholeheartedly to spiritual things. Their communion, the *Consolamentum*, was usually only offered to adherents on their death-bed. Again the interest in this different – and some still maintain heretical – form of Christianity, is growing, for it has deep spiritual, if not specifically magical, implications.

In Britain and much of northern Europe the Saxons were establishing themselves, as farmers and traders, invaders and ravishers. They brought with them their own native religions, worshipping many gods and goddesses, and bringing with them their magical Rune alphabet. Like many early writing systems, each symbol or letter had a magical importance and power. Once more the Runes, as a system of divination and magical working are coming into prominence today. Each Rune letter is the name of a god, goddess or power, divided usually into three families, each ruled by a particular deity. By making a set of Runes, carved on ash wood, sacred to Woden, it is possible to use them both for guidance and prediction. By using the angular shapes of the Runes intertwined they can become powerful talismans, directed to request the aid of particular gods with some human purpose. Although this tradition of ancient wisdom has slumbered undisturbed for many centuries in Britain and elsewhere, it has been awakened to new understanding by those who have the occult skill to unravel its mysteries, reinterpret them into modern terminology, and present them, in various forms to the students of today. Raymond Buckland, in America, has invented an entire system of Anglo-Saxon Wicca, or witchcraft, as a result of his own studies. This is not an old tradition reborn, intact; it is a modern reinvention, suited to our understanding, but it can be a potent system, none the less.

During the Middle Ages as well as the confrontations between the Church and the older country religions, surviving as pagan practices and celebrations, among the heath-dwellers, the heathens, beyond the towns' walls, much wisdom and shared knowledge was being discovered by the learned folk. Because long pilgrimages were in fashion, and because the Crusades caused soldiers and priests to stray far from their native villages, into unknown territory, towards the Holy Land, cultures met, clashed, and often intermingled to benefit both. The science of Alchemy, the Art of the Black Land, Al Khem, was first brought to Britain from Egypt and Arabia, and from that developed the modern sciences of chemistry and physics. Astronomers beneath the clear skies over the deserts gave the names to stars and constellations, which we in these misty northern lands use to this day: Betelgeuse, Spica, Aldabaran, Al Deneb and many more. The use of the figure zero opened up the study of mathematics which previously had been carried on clumsily with Roman numerals instead of the Arabic ones with which we are familiar today.

Alchemy is still a subject which has its researchers today working on both physical alchemical processes of refining pure gold from other metals, and on spiritual alchemy, working on their own souls, to produce their inner sacred nature, distilled from the dross of everyday living. Carl Jung was interested in the ancient writings of the alchemists, for he could detect in their coded instructions and complicated descriptions of dissolution and coagulation, psychological processes which could equally well be applied to the soul of man, as it could to chemicals and minerals. From the tangled and indefinable patterns of man's inner psyche a pure and shining spirit could be brought forth, and from the shattered inner world of the mentally disturbed could emerge, phoenix-like, the restored consciousness of the healed patient.

Like the Grail Legends, the techniques of the alchemists provide a structured journey, deeply embedded in symbolism, through which the would-be initiate can travel, to seek that shining jewel of refined spirit within him. By using the encounters with the Grail Guardians or the various chemical processes, he can test aspects of the spirit within, strengthening and refining them, until the object of his Quest is achieved. It is possible to recognise the magical processes by which one sort of thing is changed, miraculously, into some other. It is by bringing the reality of the inner levels of consciousness to work on what is available, and allowing the changes that process will cause to occur fully which will eventually complete the work of transformation, on both inner and outer levels.

From medieval roots we have the basis of many ceremonial and secret traditions, varying from the inheritance of Christian Rosenkreutz with its magical and symbolic fraternity which has active adherents in many parts of the world today, to the practices in speculative Freemasonry. In the Middle Ages there was a great increase in the erection of great churches and cathedrals, each built by masons deeply committed to preserving their secret knowledge of construction, symbolism and worship. In every old church their excellent work, their hidden marks and preserved tradition can be discovered by those who explore the fabric with open eyes. In among the carvings of the patrons of the new church were inevitably carvings of the masons themselves, and their families, there are the ancient pagan Green Men, the sacred animals, the Goddess, too, in her guise as a deer or hare or even cat, that most unchurchly creature. Within the lodges, where they drew out their plans with eye and experience, the secrets of their initiations were preserved by the Master Masons and their apprentices. The secret grips and signs and words had a value in a non-literate society where a man had to prove his ability to work on a new building by word and token, not by a modern trade union membership card. The skills were learned in practice, preserved in ritual and taught to those who followed within the Craft, wherever in Europe the work of building God's houses took them. They live on today.

With the contacts across Europe to the Holy Land, all kinds of new knowledge was gradually distributed through all the lands – knowledge of herbs and healing, magic and talismans, words of power in ancient tongues, symbols and gestures which had significance throughout half the world. The Hebrew language and its literature began to creep into the libraries of the learned, and its magical applications through Gematria, the secret numerical interpretation of Hebrew letters, which gave even simple phrases a potent concealed meaning. Grimoires, the magical grammars, books of elaborate ritual instructions were published, and copies of them found their way all over Europe. The Key of Solomon is still in print today, with its pictures of magical instruments, sigils, talismans and symbolism, the complex rites of invisibility, spells for finding wealth underground, and making the dead reveal their secrets. Complicated systems of magical training were written down, one of the most famous being *The Book of Abra Melin the Mage*, which details the six months of prayer, magical actions, purification and offerings, all within strictly controlled limits. A special terrace covered with river sand had to be prepared, as well as particular garments, an altar, incenses and prayers, which had to be said at prescribed times of day. The object of this period of dedication and prayer was in order to have conversation with your Holy Guardian Angel. The prayers and fasting had to be performed exactly, because, unlike modern magical work, which is performed within a cleansed and sealed circle, there was no defence prepared against unpleasant entities or influences. This Aleister Crowley and others have found to their cost, for the magical process can easily leave you open and unprotected from evil influences unless the purification and withdrawal from the world is followed exactly. Modern students have tried to replicate the work of Abra Melin the Mage, in his detailed instructions to his Son, with varying results.

In the Middle Ages, too, the study of Qabalah, the Hebrew system of mystical revelation, based on the familiar glyph of the Tree of Life, began their expansion among the magically inclined scholars of the time. Qabalah means roughly, 'From Mouth to Ear', so, like the teaching of the Druids and many a secret priesthood before them, it is an oral teaching which was not intended to be passed on in written form, but learned by heart, meditated on, and debated between teacher and pupils. It is not a religion, but the ten spheres of the Tree of Life do represent the coming into manifestation of the power of God, flowing down from Kether, the Crown, through Chokmah and Binah, Chesed and Geburah, Tiphareth, Netzach and Hod, Yesod into Malkuth, the Kingdom of Earth. There are plenty of excellent books dealing with varying aspects of this Mystery, for it is one of the most important serious studies for any student today. Nearly all lodges of ceremonial magicians owe something to the study and under-standing of Qabalah, even if it is only the art of pathworking, which originally derived from working with the symbolism of the paths linking pairs of spheres on the Tree of Life. It does provide a safe if complex and detailed framework upon which all manner of magical activities may be built.

The Tree of Life may be used as a flow-chart of power from heaven to earth, and as such has had the Tarot trumps, astrologi-cal attributions, colours, numbers, almost all pantheons of gods and goddesses, and every possible divination system related to it at some time. Certainly it will act as a universal hat-rack for all the sets of symbols which can be fitted on to its ten pegs (eleven counting Daath, the hidden sphere from which the earth fell from its former place in creation), but that was not its original purpose. Rather it was a ladder by which mankind could climb back to its own previously elevated position, stepping up through each of the ten stages towards perfection. These same ten steps were used to signify the grades of initiation within such organisations as the Hermetic Order of the Golden Dawn, which flourished in Eng-land at the end of the nineteenth century, and into the early twentieth. Fragments of its well-documented rituals are still in use today, in various guises, both in Britain and in America. The vast tome in which Israel Regardie published the rituals, the training exercises and divinatory arts has been reprinted many times, and makes a positive museum of useful and fascinating information. If you happen to have a group of ten friends, you can act out the ceremonies as they are printed, for they provide ample ritual practice.

Another aspect of magic which was explored by members of the Golden Dawn, both in its heyday, and in smaller groups since, is the work on Enochian magic. This is a system discovered in the sixteenth century by Dr John Dee, Queen Elizabeth I's astrologer and chief spy. Working with Edward Kelley as his scryer, he was shown a number of complicated tables, rather like crossword puzzle blanks, without any black squares, upon which letters of an arcane alphabet were written. It is said by some commentators that this was actually the language of Atlantis, from which many modern occult groups trace a descent of their knowledge. Kelley would see these tables in his black scrying glass or a small crystal ball (both of which are on show in the British Museum, in London, together with protective wax talismans, and other esoteric equipment), and an angel would instruct him by pointing out letters, in reverse order, which he then dictated to Dr Dee, who wrote down these archaic messages.

Scholars still debate the origins and reality of Enochian as a language, some agreeing with Dr Dee, that it was the tongue of the angels in heaven, and named after the prophet Enoch, others saying it was a spies' code, and others attributing it to much more ancient sources on Atlantis. Other people, both before Dee and since, have received messages in this strange alphabet, and it does occasionally turn up in dreams and visions. As a magical system, Enochian is used in a powerful form of invocation, called the Enochian Calls, where the language is pronounced, letter by letter, in a special way, to request particular help from Spirits and Angels. There is also a form of Enochian chess which is played using pieces in the form of Egyptian gods, and requires four players, one of whom may be an angel. Although there are a number of books which explain this system it is not really one that should be recommended to beginners, as it is very tempting to try out the calls, or Aethyrs, and the results can be extremely powerful and are unpredictable even in the hands of experts.

There are all kinds of exponents of magical systems, both ancient and modern, and practitioners follow all kinds of paths, from that of the solo hermit, living and working totally alone, to those fortunate members of the large schools and lodges of contemporary ceremonial magic. Another whole class of students of the Mysteries include all the various types of witches. The last 'Witchcraft Act' was repealed in Britain as recently as 1951, and replaced with a law against fraudulent mediums who con people out of money for predictions. Immediately that happened a number of witches began to emerge from their secret past and began to expound their theories and make known their practices to an expectant world. Some were publicity-seekers; others were inheritors of an ancient tradition. Some mixed together gleaned fragments from a variety of pagan sources from all over Europe.

One of the foremost of them was Gerald Gardner, a retired

customs officer, who having returned after many years in the Far East, found in the south of England some people who claimed to practise witchcraft. In time he was initiated by them and learned something of their secrets, their festival celebrations, arts and rituals. Having published a novel which was not a literary success on the theme of witchcraft, Gerald Gardner began to share his discoveries with others by publishing *Witchcraft Today*, shortly followed by *The Meaning of Witchcraft*. In these he sets out a whole system involving High Priestesses and High Priests, a cycle of seasonal festivals, initiation into three degrees, an idea almost certainly borrowed at some stage from that other Craft, the Freemasons, and the lists of ceremonial equipment which are still frequently described in books on witchcraft today. How much of his work, based on the arts of covens of witches living and performing their festivals, their healing rites and their spells, sky-clad, can be proven to be the Old Religion as it was always practised in Britain, is debatable. It is known that many of the beautiful prayers and chants were written in the 1950s by Doreen Valiente, and that other parts of the Gardnerian Tradition have been derived from Italy and other parts of Europe. As a magical system it has brought a lot of joy and fun to many people, who can trace their initiation back through various High Priestesses and High Priests to Gardner's own coven, which still exists and meets regularly in Britain today.

The Gardnerian system of witchcraft spawned many imitators and descendants of various degrees of directness, one of the most written about being the Alexandrian tradition, springing not from Alexandria, but from the works of Alex Sanders. He claimed to have received his knowledge direct from his grandmother, although his known family history shows that both his grandmothers were dead by the time he was 7 years old! Also, despite claiming different roots, most of his rituals and practices were those as described in the Gardnerian *Book of Shadows*, with minor variations. Stuart Farrar, who first came across witchcraft when he was writing for one of the popular Sunday papers, and his wife Janet, have written several books expounding Alex's system with their own additions, bringing this subject to an ever wider audience.

There has always been a ghostly system called 'Traditional Witchcraft' whose followers are few and far between, holding that their knowledge has to be limited to the family, and of outsiders only those who marry into it or are adopted ritually may have any right to the secret feasts and arts. Where information about this tradition has come to light it shows a totally different approach. There are no High Priests or Priestesses, no degrees, and members of the family, of all ages, act out a cycle of seasonal ritual plays which mime the magical progress of the Goddess and her Lord through the natural agricultural year. Unlike the Gardnerian and Alexandrian rituals, the Goddess and her consort do not have the borrowed names of Italian deities, but titles appropriate to the season of the year, or function, according to the rite.

Beneath this runs yet another ancient hidden form of the Craft, that of the solo village witch, serving her community as healer, herbalist, diviner, talisman-maker and leader of the village's feasts and festivals, bringing a secret magic to their Harvest Home, the sowing and reaping of corn, the husbandry and killing of meat animals. Here is a truly hidden tradition, and those who preserved it shied away, and still do, from the term 'witch' and yet it was probably these old dames or Cunning Men who were the targets for the witch-finders of the Inquisition. If their psychic skills were as good as their knowledge of herbs and poisons, no doubt most of them escaped their persecutor's clutches. It is only today, when the idea of Shamanism is attracting so much attention, that people are looking for traces of it within their own culture. In Britain the preservation of Old Lore, of the Old Religion, of the Old Ways, was probably in the hands of such individuals or their families. There is no evidence of actual covens existing in Britain at any time before this century. It certainly would have been recorded in the witch trials if any had really been discovered. Although Margaret Murray makes a case for it in her books, she did make some enormous leaps in the dark when it came to what witches were supposed to have done. Again, there are modern covens who look to her works for guidance, and practise what she preached in her historical expositions.

There are many other paths of magical descent which are being followed with a greater or lesser degree of historical backing. Those of healer or diviner, of shaman, borrowing from the known or invented ideas of the Red Indian or Siberian medicine man, or of any other type of practitioner of the hidden arts, all have their reborn followers and would-be initiates. In some cases there is a genuine line of ancient knowledge, passed down through many Western cultures in a fairly pure and unsullied form; in other instances there is no real evidence of what the older practitioners did or believed. There is, sadly, little evidence for the unbroken lines of secret wisdom, stretching back to Classical times, or even earlier. However, those who are trained and effective in the skills of time-travel, of escaping the limitations of a one-life only existence, and who have mastered the art of reliving previous lives, rediscovering old knowledge and skill have been able to penetrate the veils of time and erosion and filled their cups of knowledge at the original spring, returning with old wisdom, reborn, in memory and heart.

CHAPTER SEVEN

The Path of the Hearth Fire

We do not all aspire to become shamans, magicians or mystics – for
most of us the duty is to fulfil our vocation within the boundaries of a
job, home and family. But something of a collective responsibility is
being felt more generally – call it a pressure from the Otherworld to
an inner evolution. The way to inner, spiritual growth is greatly
desired, and though many methods are available, not all are suitable
or practical. ... The inner guardian is the initiator for each of us.

Caitlin and John Matthews, THE WESTERN WAY VOL. I

In Dion Fortune's description, the 'Path of the Hearth Fire' is one
where the Seeker, after acknowledging the power of the Mysteries, is expected to turn his or her back on that path for this life at
least. It is the difficult choice that has to be made. Sometimes that
is the best option, particularly if you have many other commitments on your time or energy. Bringing up a young family,
holding down a powerful job, teaching or researching, or many
kinds of activities where one hundred per cent effort is required
will, for the time being, mean that the occult path should be left
alone.

Another reason for tracing a mundane way is in the sad event of an occult student suffering any kind of mental disturbance, which, statistics state, can affect one in fourteen of the population. Magical practices will seldom be the cause of such a breakdown, although anyone who deliberately tries to work against the Laws of Order may find mental instability is one of the side-effects. Because most magical acts have at least half their power in realms of the mind and controlled consciousness it should be obvious that if the mind is disturbed then that essential control is lost, and no magical act can be performed safely. Mental distress also unbalances the patient's judgement, and he may feel he is under psychic attack, because the smooth responses achieved from meditation are no longer there, and disturbing images and sensations take their place. If any sort of mental disorder should happen to affect you during your training, it is important firstly to stop all magical work, meditation and particularly any kind of banishing rituals or psychic defence work, and secondly to inform your tutor. You will then be granted six months or a year of mundane work so that you can become totally restabilised, and perhaps then you will be ready to continue.

Even if your condition is being treated by a doctor, and appears to be under control, you are a danger to yourself, when your vulnerable subtle levels of consciousness are exposed, whatever the original cause. Treatment by tranquillisers or other prescribed drugs is not the same as a cure. In fact many of the drugs which are prescribed as anti-depressants, or as sleeping pills, or even pick-up pills have serious effects upon the psyche. It is possible to see this because the pattern of the pill-taker's aura is often observed to be vibrating as they are knocked half-way out of their bodies by the treatment. The addictive nature of these drugs is only just being admitted by the medical profession, and sadly, there are many people, who were prescribed tranquillisers for a valid medical reason, who are just as hooked on their daily dose as the sad folk addicted to heroin or cocaine.

If you are involved in any kind of magical training or work then you should avoid taking any kind of drug, and should you be unfortunate enough to suffer from some condition which makes continuous medication necessary, then you should consult your magical instructor as to what you should do. In many cases it is possible to consult an alternative therapist who may be able to relieve your complaint by non-drug methods, or use forms of healing which restore your control over your body or mind, gently and fully. It is important to remain in good health during magical training, giving up bad habits like smoking and any kind of drug-taking, and restricting the amount of alcohol you imbibe. The work is hard, it requires all those sensitive areas of your perceptions and sensations to be fully under your control, even if you are only looking at the Tarot cards, or performing a healing spell for someone else. You will find it extremely hard to heal others if you are not well, and it is imperative that you recognise that your health is your own responsibility, physical and mental, and that you should do everything within your power to maintain it, by reasonable diet, exercise, rest and as clean an environment as you can manage. If all these factors are against you, then perhaps you should work to improve your situation before continuing with other esoteric work.

Sometimes it is necessary to turn your back upon the desirable occult road until you have completed your life's work in the world. Some people write to me and say they are forty or fifty or sixty and is it too old to begin to learn magic? The answer is 'Of course not!' If you are ready as a mature, or even quite old person, to begin the hard task of inner and outer study, the chances are that you will have developed many of the necessary talents so your progress will be much swifter than that of some young students, only in their twenties. Magic requires patience, it requires long periods of concentration, it needs students to be able to solve problems, discover meanings to complex puzzles, and to make sense of ancient or legendary material. Most of those kinds of skills are mastered during years of work, or rearing a family and making a home. Older people know their own limitations, they recognise when they can take short-cuts safely, they have self-confidence, and once they have made a dedication to any project they will see it through to the end.

The allocation of time and energy to magical work is another art. Quite a lot of it goes on all the time, and it is imperative to recognise that esoteric work, witchcraft or what have you is not a hobby, to be taken up now and again when there is nothing good on television. Whether or not you undergo a specific initiation into a magical group, your commitment is total, for those who play at being witches or occultists are like children running races along a motorway. Sooner or later the forces with which they are interacting will get in their way, and they will be spiritually flattened, just as they would if they fell under a truck. This is not the work of evil forces, but is a constant law, like gravity. If you step off a high building then gravity will bring you swiftly to the ground. If you call upon the vast forces which move the universe and then ignore them, they will carry you away, just as you cannot turn the tide to suit yourself, or switch off the current in a river. The forces, once set in motion, will run their course, and it is wise to be prepared.

Because much of magical work, the intuitive processes of inner teaching, and the energies by which your spells are made to work run through a different level of reality you may be unaware that anything is going on for much of the time. It is for that reason that you are instructed to attend to your dreams and visions, and find time every day for meditation. In these periods of calm it is possible to review what is happening beneath the surface, and gain insight, direction and practical help with whatever projects you are working on. Spells and ritual aims are like seeds. If the ground is well prepared, in that you have decided exactly what you are trying to achieve, have given a good deal of thought to the best way to bring it about, and have sensibly sorted out the most effective symbolism, correspondences and so on, then the seed of that desire will grow swiftly into reality, bringing health, hope or information to you. You are also wise to ask that whatever you receive will come to you in a way that you will recognise, and in a manner which does not scare the wits out of you. This may seem obvious, but it is sometimes overlooked by the enthusiastic novice who asks for power and gets it! Remember, spells work!

There is often a period of time after the ritual has been completed when nothing seems to happen. In a properly conducted rite there ought to be time at the end for all participants to sit and listen, or focus on the purpose of the working once again, briefly, and see what response, positive or negative, they get. The inner will always give a 'yea' or 'nay' if asked. Even so, it may be days or weeks or months before the spell finally works into the physical world. By then, if you have gone about your work correctly, you will have forgotten all about it, so it can come as a bit of a shock when your desire is suddenly fulfilled. The seed of that desire will have been growing secretly, undisturbed by being dug up and examined every day. Your dreams and meditations will bring you hints that all is well, and that your aim is progressing properly and that should be enough.

Whichever path towards the Mysteries you pursue it will be a lonely path, for although you might be in a position to share certain festivals with a coven, or join in the works of a lodge, the rest of the time you will have to be living your mundane life, in the home and among your family and friends; in the office or workplace among colleagues whose interests probably lie in other directions; or around the ordinary folk whom you encounter in shops and whilst travelling. From many of these people you will feel cut off, not because you believe what you are studying is wrong, but because they may not be able to understand your interest, might ridicule your magical practices, or consider what you are involved in is inherently evil. Too much media attention has been given to those who claim to be black magicians. Real black magicians do not advertise, they are too busy designing nastier germ warfare materials, bigger and more devastating nuclear bombs, better ways of causing starvation to millions, than getting their faces and anti-evolutionary views into the popular press. Black magic is not a task for amateurs: to succeed with working with the forces of destruction and chaos you have to be many times more careful in order to avoid the inevitable backlash.

At present there are few residential schools of magic, although in many parts of the country occasional weekend or short midweek courses do occur. There are a few places where it is possible to arrange a mystical retreat, so that students can get to know their real desires, experience the loneliness of individual enlightenment, and seek repose from the frantic activities of the mundane world. However, if you take your meditation practices seriously, these will provide a small haven of peace in even the most hectic day. Later on you might be able to arrange a sort of holiday at home, if you can get the place to yourself throughout a weekend or longer, and make that a time of self-dedication, reassessment and preparation for a new phase, at least once a year. Such a simple retreat from the world can be very rewarding and worthwhile, allowing you to recharge your mental and spiritual batteries. No doubt places for actual pagan spiritual retirement will be established, although a quiet off-peak holiday in the countryside could bring just as much benefit, if the time and solitude is used properly.

If you dedicate yourself to magical work, you can attempt the Path of the Hearth Fire, where you live fully in the world, acknowledging and fulfilling your mundane life as well as esoteric commitments, but you will have a hard task. In earlier ages, those who were fully committed to the esoteric way of life were often in a different situation, having sufficient money or family support to be able to pursue their studies without the added complication of a day-to-day job, or conventional family commitments. At the turn of the century, when the Hermetic order of the Golden Dawn was in its heyday, and other serious practitioners of magic were making progress in teaching and enriching the esoteric wisdom of the West, most of these people were wealthy. Many of them were very well educated, being able to read ancient magical texts in Latin and Greek, also in Hebrew, Arabic and many of the other ancient languages. Scholarship had unravelled the mysteries of Egyptian Hieroglyphic writing, and others were reading the magical texts, some of which were 5,000 years old from Chaldea, by unlocking the secrets of cuneiform.

Today we suffer from a different handicap in esoteric studies, for rather than having to decipher material written in Runes or Linear B we are overwhelmed with the amount of literature there is in our own language. Texts from Egypt, Greece, Rome, India, Chaldea, Ireland and all over Europe have now been translated and are published for us to read, if we have the time and energy to study them. Computers, fax machines, photocopiers and all the modern technological hardware have provided us with so much material that many students are so swamped that they do not know where to begin. Taken together with the fact that few people are in a position to devote their entire lives to study and practice of the arcane arts, it makes progress just as difficult for modern occultists as it was for our Victorian predecessors.

Some people approach the occult as a way out of the difficulties of their ordinary lives, expecting that magical skills can be acquired easily and quickly, and having such powers will immediately sort out their love life, supply them instantly with plenty of money, a comfortable home, success in business or in passing examinations, or gaining entry to any élite society into which they wish to insinuate themselves. The truth is a very different matter. The pursuit of occult wisdom will first of all cause the Seeker to come face to face with himself, without the protection of his rose-coloured spectacles. He will have to examine his relationships with those around him, his family, his beloved, and all those with whom he has any dealings in his occupation. There is no magic charm, no love potion which will grant anyone the love they desire but do not deserve. There is no spell which will bring instant wealth except as a result of many years of hard work in the real world. There is no initiation which will grant wisdom without it being earned, life after life, by genuine effort and dedication, no matter what might be said in novels or magazine articles. Magic requires real, hard, consistent work. You can't buy power for money, you can't sacrifice anything for it, except your own time and energy. You can't buy understanding with blood or tears or suffering. What you will encounter, as you work your way deeper into the labyrinth is a greater awareness of what you are and what you can become. You will discover skills and abilities and capacities that you never imagined you might possess. These things are yours alone, part of your unexplored birthright, and they can be expanded to an enormous degree.

It certainly might be the case that having discovered what is really required to turn you into a successful magician or witch you decide that the commitment is too much, that the time, the effort and the dedication required are more than you can reasonably spare at the moment. Be strong enough to admit this, if only to yourself. It will never be too late to begin your training, when you have more time, and if you have tried some of the exercises. like meditation and the study of mythology, the calmness that the first produces will always be useful, and the ability to concentrate is a valuable asset in any walk of life. There are many aspects of occultism which can reasonably be fitted into a crowded life, even if you only allow yourself one evening a month to attend a lecture, or the time to read one relevant book.

The other approach is to acknowledge your continuing desire to come to an understanding of the Mysteries, and accept that you will have a twin path in life. This is the situation for the greatest percentage of all students and more experienced practitioners of the Western Mystery Tradition. Each of us has a home and family, a full-time, mundane job, all the ordinary commitments of mortgages, ongoing education and the social interactions of the rest of the population. On top of that we have our esoteric practices, our dedications to the school, lodge or society for which we have to spare time. Lectures or other training materials have to be prepared for our students, and sometimes overseas visits to run workshops or seminars have to be fitted into a crowded schedule. Very few of Britain's most active occult teachers are free to commit their life entirely to pursuing their inner-life interests. We all have, from time to time, to choose between one set of commitments and another.

Today the Path of the Hearth Fire is not necessarily one in

which all occult work is abandoned. Sometimes it is necessary to divide your time between those things to which you have an ongoing association: your job, your relationships with family and children, the outside world, and the matters of the spirit and your quest for enlightenment. You must not allow the attraction and enchantment of occult things to cause you to divert your energies from the real world, as perceived by ordinary folk. Magic is not for escapists, for people who want to get rid of their commitments to humanity, for failures, for people who cannot cope with relationships, or who expect it to be possible to wave a magic wand and have all their problems solved for them instantly. It is not a short-cut to fame or riches, for the work required to be a successful occultist is far greater than that required to become a company director or business big-wig. There are few rich witches or magicians in the twentieth century, although they may have vast stores of spiritual wealth, the gold of personal experience, health, happiness and inner peace, which the cut-throat world of enterprise would deny them.

Unless you can understand what your aims in life are, and work through them logically and sequentially, your esoteric studies will have no firm foundation. It is important to be able to form genuine friendships with people, to develop loving and caring partnerships, to respect and understand your parents and their wishes for you. It is vital that you provide an emotionally warm and safe environment for your children, so that they may grow up into balanced human beings. Those who practise extremes of pagan religion or put their magical exercises before the needs of others in their homes will not permit their youngsters to grow up uninfluenced by their extreme views. Children are naturally very sensitive to psychic atmospheres and will recognise that magical things are going on all around them. They should not have their parents' religious, dietary or philosophical views rammed down their throats from an early age, nor should they have to suffer the embarrassment of knowing that their parents are 'witches', or 'have secrets' that they must not talk about at school. Certainly, a loving relationship and an openness about simple festivals which may be celebrated in their homes or gardens will intrigue children. If it is gently explained to them, in words and terms they fully understand, that their parents follow a different religion to some people, that they carry out work for healing or helping people in a special way, then those young ones will grow up appreciating what is going on. Later on, they may choose the esoteric path for themselves, or adhere to a more mundane one. The children of magicians and witches do not necessarily become occult students, just as many of the most dedicated occult folk around have perfectly orthodox parents and a normal upbringing. We are all really children of our own previous incarnations, as much as we are genetically children of our physical parents. Nevertheless, it is important to recognise that sane and caring relationships, or friendships with those around you are signs of the successful magician. If many of those acquaintances have no notion that the individual concerned is a witch, or magician, it is so much better for all concerned. The most infuriating occult students are those who boast of the secrets they know but may not talk about, the special meetings they attend, the hidden conclaves of which they are a part, but from which outsiders are excluded. Silence and discretion are great virtues.

Because the patterns of relationships are changing, the backgrounds of people coming to study the Mysteries are producing different situations, which have to be discussed and accepted or rejected by the occult fraternities. From the Victorian era, when large families were the fashion, and when many people kept servants, lived in large mansions, and had vast sums of inherited wealth to draw on, to the modern situation of individuals, who live alone in small flats or bedsitters, or are part of a much smaller household, living in compact new houses, things have changed a lot. Certainly few of the Victorian servants would have had much knowledge of spiritual matters, outside their orthodox church services. Few of the factory workers, those in mining and industry, or any of the dull, tedious and heavy jobs of their age would have any knowledge of the eternal verities, nor much opportunity to learn about them, yet small flames were kept burning. From those struggling Victorian grandparents and great-grandparents have grown up whole generations of liberated and aware individuals.

The two World Wars changed the shape of society on one level, and the development of the new technologies, the media, the instant worldwide communications systems and the way people are educated have produced a new race of humanity in the Western world, at least. Within this new generation not only are there entirely different patterns of living, working and homemaking, but education, access to information, better food and housing have all contributed to a healthier, better informed and freer kind of people. It is necessary that the forms of magical practices which are being formulated today, and the way they are made available to the many students who have grown up in this vastly changed world, are suited to their understanding and desires. It is for this reason that thinking teachers of the occult arts are radically altering what they teach, how they teach, and to whom this instruction is made available.

In Victorian times, anyone who did not adhere to the moral, religious or philosophical mores of the time was banned from entry to magical orders and there are still senior occult fraternities who stick firmly to these old-fashioned rules. In other branches of the esoteric world, groups and schools are being founded on totally new bases. There are many more women, for example, taking high office in ceremonial magic groups, whereas in the last generation Dion Fortune was treading a very lonely road. Certainly, Orders like the Golden Dawn did admit women at all levels, but the methods of working were patriarchal, based to a considerable extent on higher aspects of Freemasonry, and drawing on Hebrew and Egyptian sources of wisdom and symbolism. Although this work continues today in a number of societies and schools, as well as independent lodges, it is important to recognise that more and more students are treading a solo path, or one with a small group meeting in a domestic setting, rather than the elaborate permanent set-up of a ritual temple.

Magic is a meritocracy. You will rise through the ranks of a lodge at a speed which depends on your own efforts and successes at the various training exercises. Ceremonial groups tend not to be democratic, but because they are made up of trained psychics, individuals are chosen to fill particular roles depending on their ability to do so, rather than how long they have been initiates. Orders can be extremely strict about their trainees' activities, insisting that no other magical commitments are undertaken whilst they are working with that particular lodge. This is a sensible idea, because, as has been said before, magical groups do develop group souls and these in turn affect those who are under their aegis. If a novice joins several groups at once the combined influences of several group souls can be totally disruptive and uncomfortable for him, and his inner work would be impossible.

If you are unable to accept discipline and continuous hard work within such a lodge and feel it would be easier on your own, where you will not have the distraction of power struggles and limitation on your outside activities, you will soon discover that this is not necessarily so. The group will be supportive and will provide a structured training programme, and the regular contact with others at various levels on their magical path will spur you on. However, such lodges are fairly rare, and only a small proportion of Seekers are admitted even to the basic training. It also depends on how close you live to the cities where such groups meet as to whether you might be accepted, if you make contact. Another rule which denies some people membership of particular groups is that of sexual orientation. If you are an ordinary married individual, or a single person with heterosexual preferences, you would be acceptable to any lodge, but there are quite a few which have rules against admitting practising homosexuals, and their questionnaires ask specific questions about this matter.

On the other hand, particularly in America, there are a number of mainly pagan or Wiccan organisations which are specifically for gay people. There is a form called Dianic witchcraft for women and lesbians and a Faery Tradition for homosexual men. There may be similar groups in Britain although, like all esoteric groups, you have to look out for details as there are no entirely comprehensive directories or annual lists of societies and schools. If you are a homosexual you may have exactly the same sort of misunderstandings with your partner as heterosexual folk do. Magic requires a commitment to the work, and a dedication to the people involved, which is often greater than any ordinary relationship can stand. Also, because much magical work has to be done alone, or in secret, it can cause rifts and difficulties which are seldom spelled out in the literature. There will always be the disappearances to meetings, the acquisition of strange, seemingly outlandish paraphernalia, the scent of burning incense or joss-sticks which not everyone likes, which those who share your home, whatever your relationship to them may be, will have to have explained to them.

Some organisations, however, have always been one-sex groups. Ordinary 'Blue' freemasonry has always been a 'men-only' society, but there is an Order of Women Freemasons, which is all women, and there is also the International Order of Co-Masons which is open to both men and women. These are not the sort of organisations which you simply apply to join, although in some instances advertisements for new members are placed in certain journals. If you are interested it is best to try to find some members of the society you wish to join and find out about it from them. They may well be able to get to know you and sponsor your application. Some of these types of societies, and those based on Rosicrucian principles, may have quite expensive fees, for meetings, or training, or publications, etc., so do find out before you commit yourself to any group. This same question should be asked of any magical training school, coven or fellowship, for some do have regular subscriptions, or dues for meetings, expensive regalia or batches of instructional material. As these can all be long-term commitments, from a year or so of basic training to a life-long association, you ought to discover what your financial outlay is likely to be in order to budget.

Essentially, any path through the labyrinth you may choose to take will be a difficult one. Magic is *not easy*. The achievement of the kind of power which can reshape the universe is not earned lightly, there are no short-cuts, nor can the paying of high fees gain you anything except perhaps an overdraft! No one can learn for you, give you powers or degrees you have not genuinely earned by months of hard effort. No one can interpret your dreams for you, solve your problems, sort out your relationships and sexual preferences. No one can love you if you do not love and respect yourself. If you cannot love yourself, how can you expect anyone else to love you? Ultimately any magical training has got to work on the person you are to begin with. If you have certain aims in life, then one path through the maze may lead more directly to that goal than another. If you happen to be a homosexual, then, if you admit this, certain societies or traditions will not accept you. If you wish to be part of many sorts of groups or societies then some that you might like to join will not permit you to belong to several, so you will have to choose. Following one path at a time, as a novice, is certainly the safest and most rewarding.

You will need to look hard and long at what you are, where you have come from on your spiritual path, and where you most desire to go. It is a painful and lonely way, but you alone have access to all the details of your adventures, your hopes and plans, your successes and failures, and it is from these scattered fragments that you will have to build the new you, the magical self, the competent occultist. The more certain you are of who you are to begin with, the greater can be your progress. It is useless to sweep your faults under the carpet, for they will grow and expand and eventually trip you. You cannot escape your background, your roots or your sexual inclinations. You may well be able to change these given time and dedication, but you must accept what you are at first.

You must also accept where you are in the real, solid, boring and mundane world. You cannot wave a magic wand and get an excellent job with a high salary and all the perks. Certainly you can work a spell on yourself to become the most effective and far-thinking engineer in your town or the best word-processor operator, but you also have to put in the hours at the drawing board and computer keyboard. You can have any job or desire you are capable of, but you will have to sacrifice hobbies, friendships and other activities to get it. Most real magicians have totally satisfying jobs which supply enough money for them to live comfortably though not lavishly, they have large circles of friends, both occult and ordinary, play sport well enough to enjoy it, have happy and enduring family relationships or marriages, with children, or from their own choice, live alone, dedicating much of their time and part of their homes to magical work.

The skills which true esoteric dedication will grant you will have uses in the home and workplace just as they do in the temple or circle. The ability to get on with people, share projects and serve the needs of others is just as important and will work as well in lodge as in the family home. The ability to see into the future will help with holiday plans and employment prospects. Healing skills work on yourself, your family and friends and the whole Earth, if they are learned thoroughly, understood and properly applied to the situation in hand, whatever it may be. The awareness of the other levels of existence, the source worlds where plans may be formulated before they grow forth into the light of day can be as helpful in designing new work ventures as it can in looking at long-term occult projects. Each new skill and acquired craft has both a mundane and magical application. The more competent a human being you are the better both worlds will become for you.

In every field of your life, your health, your home, your family and friends, your job and your magical life will all benefit from the calmness, the self-confidence and the ongoing awareness which develop as you master meditation, understand symbolism, learn to apply the varied arts of magical work, divination and healing. These techniques may seem a long way from the every-day world, yet all have real uses in the shops, on a train or among your co-workers if you allow your growing senses of psychic impressions or far-seeing to be applied all the time. Occult work is not a hobby, to be taken up and set aside like carpentry. It is a full-time commitment which has all manner of advantages once it is accepted as an effective system. You can use magic to protect your house or car from break-ins, you can use it to track down a rare book or a parking space in a crowded city. You can perceive the outcome of any activity through divination, or discover your own hidden talents through astrology.

At some point you will have to choose, either the solo path, followed at your own pace, in your own way, under the strict regulations of self-discipline, sitting beside your own hearth or having the courage, for the time being, to turn your back on the occult path, allowing that vital time of healing from mental disturbance, from sadness or worldly stresses, knowing that a year or two of recuperation will be rewarded in the end. You might choose to follow a particular path, among a mixed batch of co-workers, or people of your own sex, recognising the power of attraction within magical groups, the closeness of that kind of relationship, and finding those who feel harmonious to you. To outsiders it is impossible to explain the nature of brotherhood and companionship within a magical working situation. Certainly it should not replace the mundane links with family and friends, and any groups which discourage these links should be avoided, but association with others within the lodge or coven must be given its proper place. You cannot gain respect, honour, or love without being worthy; joining an occult group will not automatically pile these upon you. You may encounter power struggles, hierarchical battles, being overlooked for a magical position you covet, having to work closely with people you may not actually like in the outside world – but these are all parts of the process of magical working.

Within the privacy of your own home, and inside your own head where there is potentially vast space and whole galaxies of worlds which you can create to your design, there is a special haven to which you can return day by day to rediscover yourself. Work slowly through your life, year by year, success by success and failure by failure. Accept each unique facet of your own character, acknowledge its value, accept the lessons it has taught you. Examine your body. Feel it, caress it and treat it gently, feed it healthy food, heal it by safe and natural methods, learn to love it, whatever shape, size and weight it may be. Discover for yourself, or in the arms of a loving partner, those places which give a thrill when stroked; have an energising massage now and again if possible; practise regular deep breathing, and fast walking for exercise. Teach your body to relax fully, allowing you to become 'bodiless' and untroubled by its needs. Learn to slip free of time and space to a personal inner world, where you can build the universe of the future to your own desire, and fill it with all those things you most long for.

Recognise not only your own needs but those of your family and workmates. Learn to share your time and energy between the enchanting magical opportunities and the ordinary activities, between your brethren in the lodge or coven and the other folk in your life. Balance carefully your need for self and the needs of others, being willing to turn aside from your own wishes to help and care for those around you. Discover just how much time and effort you need to devote to your studies every day, how often you are expected to attend meetings, what other commitments on your time and financial resources there are. It will be possible to decide if the Path of the Hearth Fire is a necessity now, if your health or the needs of those to whom you owe a natural duty demand it. There will always be another chance, later in this life or in another, to follow the fascination of the magical way when conditions will allow you the freedom to go in that direction.

CHAPTER EIGHT

A Passage through the Inner Worlds

But as the passage presents no hindrance
To the spirit unappeased and peregrine
Between two worlds become much like each other,
So I find words I never thought to speak
In streets I never thought I should revisit
When I left my body on a distant shore.

T. S. Eliot, LITTLE GIDDING

To the outsider, magic and witchcraft appear to be fascinating subjects, involving interesting people in strange and outlandish arts, often performing these in mysterious robes or even 'sky-clad'. There seems to be a short-cut to power which will transform every aspect of someone's life for the better, ensuring a well-paid job, a desirable partner, success and even fame, certainly glamour and many advantages. The truth of the matter, in reality, is that an adept, after many years of very hard, often boring and repetitive work, will gain mental skills which indeed transform his world, but only gradually, and often in ways which benefit the whole community rather than the individual magician. He will be a well-liked and respected member of his community, and it is unlikely that his next-door neighbours or his colleagues at work will have any idea that he is actively involved with the Mysteries. His home will be welcoming, his family and friends will be healthy and widely read people, good company, but they are unlikely to be rich, or in any accepted sense powerful.

Novels and films give the impression that rituals are continuously being performed in lavishly furnished temples, where wonderful people in fabulous robes offer strange invocations amid swirling incense smoke. Fiction implies that there are numerous secret societies meeting in many cities where masked initiates compel demons and angels to do their bidding by words of power and mystic sigils. Wizards are seen, particularly in science fiction films, battling with cosmic forces for the souls of the world, and fighting off evil emperors, mighty dragons and dark forces, which exist in the universe to combat good and evolutionary progress. They never film the characters sitting quietly in their armchairs, with their eyes shut, silently meditating on some eternal matter, but, in reality, that is far more often what it is like. Certainly the adept may be working for the benefit of the Earth, for the healing of the planet's pollution, and the greening of the Wasteland, but about 75 per cent of his magic will be done inside his trained mind.

Through learning to control your own state of consciousness it is possible to switch into the level of reality wherein all the world as we know it has its cosmic roots. It is within the level of creation that all effective magic has to work. By entering the alternate planes of the inner realms it is possible to discover what the Divine Plan may be, for an individual, for a country or a whole continent. It is possible, by being in a state of awareness in which that seems to be real, not only to discover what is likely to happen, but also to make very subtle changes within the matrix of the future which in turn will alter the world. This is where the true magical power lies, and with it the enormous responsibility of knowing what you are doing is right. This only comes after many years of trial and error, usually within the confines of a contacted order, where what can and should be done is thoroughly learned, under the careful tuition of the previous generations of competent magicians.

Magic is wonderful, and fascinating, and enthralling. It is a marvellous occupation, bringing joy and success to those who persevere with their long training. It is exhilarating to be part of a working group, dressed in glorious robes, within the sacred confines of a temple not built with hands, seeing with twin vision, through the sweetly scented swirls of incense smoke, those beings from other orders of creation with whom we are working in harmony to create a better future. The sensation of shared enterprise and dedication is unparalleled, but it is something which has to be earned. The rewards are not material or financial, sometimes they are not even tangible. It is never measured by notches on your wand, nor by badges on your sleeve, but by the kind of person you have become, which will be recognised by the least psychic individual you come across in your daily life. Your self-confidence and assuredness, calmness and friendship will be seen by most of the people around you and they will know you are a 'good person' even if they have no inkling (and on the whole they shouldn't) that you are involved in magic or witchcraft.

Your companions in the lodge or coven will become your firm friends in a way which is very different from the ordinary round of acquaintances. A very special relationship, of 'Perfect Love and Perfect Trust', to quote one of the witches' ethics, is built up. Love, because unless you love first yourself, then those around you and then the whole of creation, you will have no basis for your magic. The occult arts teach service, another maxim being 'I know in order to Serve,' and it is through love of Life, the Gods or the Earth that this service is applied, using ritual, talismans, divination, healing and hard mental work. You need to trust those you make magic with because you are dealing with enormously potent forces which you may or may not be able to perceive. The others in the group should be able to see or feel them, talk with them and listen to them, and tell you what is going on, until, when your own inner senses have opened up, you are able to detect them yourself. You also need to trust your seniors and companions because all of you will be experiencing changed levels of awareness, when, unless the circle is properly cast, you are vulnerable to all kinds of errant forces. These are not evil or necessarily harmful, but they are from a different part of creation and can have very weird effects upon unprepared novices. Seeing vast angelic figures, whole rooms or even landscapes which are not those of the world you know, interacting with totem animals, guides or even inner aspects of your own soul, can be a daunting undertaking, and it is for that reason that the basic exercises which give you absolute control over your awareness are learned thoroughly.

It really is important to be able to meditate, to visualise when
you can see real pictures and to be able to enter into the other
realm during pathworkings or inner journeys. Each of these
mental skills is difficult to learn, often taking many sessions of
regular and consistent practice, spread over many months, possibly years. Essentially you are re-educating a part of your mind to
enter a half-way state between waking and sleeping, and instead
of passing through in moments, holding this poised mental
awareness for ten to sixty minutes or more. Within this ASC you
will have far more access to your memory, right through this life,
and probably into previous lives, if you bother to take time to
explore. It is from remembered scenes, passages from films or
books, even, that the images you use in magic are built up. Unless
you can remember what an oak tree looks like, you can't create
one in your imagination. Unless you have some idea what a
square is, or the colour blue, or what the number six represents,
you will have no data to build up talismans, create magical
places, and enter fully into the other levels of reality. Some of this
information will already exist inside your head, collected from all
the experiences of life. You will have seen different landscapes,
trees, buildings, museum exhibits, as well as reading about them
in illustrated books, or seeing them on TV. All this material is
there, inside your memory. You also have access to the minds of
everyone else, if you use that perception responsibly, not only
living now, but at any time in the history of mankind. You may
well have access to other minds, of animals, trees, plants, crystals
and beings from other planets, if you learn to open the doors.

Meditation requires continuous practice. You can't do it once
or twice, fail, and so give it up as a bad job. You must persist until
you can enter the relaxed physical state when your mind is
acutely alert and expansive. You will have to experiment with
any methods you come across, unless you are in the fortunate
position to have personal instruction which will ensure you gain
the knack before going on to more arcane arts. It is a knack,
something which happens when you least expect it, because play
is very much a mental state which we tend to grow out of. Serious
and determined effort will often fail when the attitude of 'Well, it
doesn't really matter, it's only a game ...' can often succeed. The
mind is more like a butterfly, to be caught in a gossamer web
rather than a hard steel trap. It is subtle, ephemeral and elusive,
but if you use a gentle approach you can capture it, intrigue it and
eventually control it. There is no certain way, which works

unfailingly for everyone – life would be much simpler if this were so, but persistence with a variety of techniques will eventually lead you to success.

You can assist your mental state by the use of quiet music: often this played on a personal stereo set can help by blotting out the sounds of the world around you, which new meditators find so disturbing. Use of a particular piece of music to trigger the state can be very useful, for you can use your personal stereo any-where, quietly, and no one is any the wiser that you are meditating. Eventually, you may be able to put away the prop, and do it for yourself. You might also find that relaxation tapes give you a good start, training those inner levels of your mind to obey and become still and aware. The use of progressive physical relaxation works well with many people, so instruction in that might be found helpful. Some people have taken to using drum-ming or chanting or striking a small bell to lead them into the correct frame of mind, others find these imported ideas disturb-ing. Whatever you do, you need to end up in a calm, relaxed state of physical stillness, when your mind and memory are aware and attentive. You need to be able to feed in data to work on without breaking your train of thought, and to be able to follow moving ideas and remember them completely. Practise on your dreams, for recalling those each day requires very much the same mental process.

To begin with, it is well worth spending a few months on regular meditation. That means at least five or six properly recorded sessions every week, not sporadic attempts at odd moments. Choose a time of day and a place, and perhaps a piece of music, or a form of deep breathing or progressive relaxation, and dedicate at least half an hour a day to the process. This allows you time to prepare, relax, meditate, record whatever you have learned, even if it doesn't seem much to begin with, have a snack, and then get on with your life. Meditation is good for you, and will produce calmness and control which is useful in most situations. Eventually you will be able to follow the progress of your thoughts through various images, concepts, pictures and received material, and then by making an effort as you go along, recalling it in full, and often expanded detail when you jot it down in your Magical Diary. Often the results of meditation do seem rather trivial, but it is the gradual build-up of mental connections which eventually lead to regular, and sometimes seemingly world-shattering, revelations. Meditation is essentially a passive process, wherein connections between memory and the need for new knowledge are made without direction or volition. You prepare a space in time, a silence and stillness to be filled with potential wisdom. The greater your distraction and playfulness, the clearer and more powerful the results. Learn to be absolutely still and poised for interlinking knowledge to flow.

The other side of this coin is the art of creative visualisation. Here you set the scene, create the landscape or the temple, welcome the gods and goddesses into your consciousness, and interact with them, again being able to recall every step of such information. It does help to make a plan, to design a talisman, sort out the items you will need for a rite before you begin it. Like the design of a drawing, the planning of a new building, the layout of engineering equipment, it has to begin in your head. Rituals have to be planned just as carefully as theatrical plays, with thought given to characters, props, scenery and furniture. In magic some of these matters remain on the mental level, although the room for a temple has to be cleansed and prepared, robes put on, incense lit, bread and wine made ready for a communion. The materials for a talisman must be found, the elements of earth, water, fire and air set out to be used in consecrating and empowering the charm. Each of these things needs to be thoroughly thought about so that it is not forgotten at the critical moment. Some things need to be blessed and dedicated to use in magical worlds, others may have to be made, or prepared in some other way.

Once you have prepared the objects for your ritual or divination or whatever, you will need to get yourself into that poised state of mind which allows you to see the past, the present and the future, all imposed upon the world you live in. Frequently in the first part of a shared ritual, the temple is created out of the mundane room, described and consecrated, and the protective angels or energies of the four quarters invoked to visible appearance (or the perception of those participating focused on that inner plane wherein these sacred beings have their real existence). This may be done as a pathworking or by everyone being led to build a set of images and symbols around the place. It is important to realise that each member of a lodge or coven has to concentrate on perceiving those shared images of guardians, gods and goddesses, or even the descent of power onto the Officers or High Priestess, according to the rite.

Although witchcraft tends to rely less upon the mental arts,

these are certainly things that the followers of the Old Religion
would have known about. Today we use the term meditation
whereas they would have mused or contemplated as they went
about the boring everyday tasks of a non-mechanised society.
Hoeing plants, spinning, weaving, hand milking, sowing corn or
reaping grain, scything hay or simply following sheep or cattle as
they roamed across the unfenced land, gave the freewheeling
mind plenty of scope to focus on other things. Those who were
naturally psychic would become aware of the activities of other
members of their close-knit communities, away at war or in the
service of their overlord. They might catch glimpses of what was
happening at the King's court, and frequently news of the death
of a queen or the birth of her child was known about in remote
villages long before the galloping messenger or crier of news
arrived. Using the forgotten parts of our brain or memory or
farsight is a skill we have tended to overlook because we rely on
books or the media to provide us with information. When no
such services existed, those who wished or needed to know had to
make use of their inherent skills. We, in the technological world,
have to relearn the essential but very difficult arts by sweat of the
brow.

Tuning into our deepest levels in quiet contemplation can be a
very rewarding activity. It is from this source that all manner of
inspiration may be encouraged to flow, whether it be that of the
poet, the singer, the musician, the creative writer, journalist,
artist, electronics wizard or chemical engineer. Inspiration is a
gift of the Goddess, whose multiple muse will enter into any mind
open and prepared to receive it. In times past initiates sought to
become princes, poets and healers through direct contact and
inspiration of one of the many goddesses. Although in some
branches of witchcraft the High Priestess and High Priest are
supposed to become overshadowed by the God and Goddess it
doesn't often happen. If you imagine trying to encompass the
forces of the seasons within a human being, or the power of a
tornado or any other of the parts of the nature of the Old Gods
you will understand that this is not what happens. Seek to be
worthy to be able to have the clear-sightedness, the dedication
and purity and some inspiring entity will surely make contact
with you, but act in an arrogant and overbearing way towards
these mighty beings of other levels of creation and you will be in
for all sorts of trouble. We have neither the right nor the power to
command anyone, human, elemental, or angelic, we can only

seek them out and politely request help, guidance or healing. To usurp the place of gods and to pretend we are capable of their energies is foolish.

You need to be able to create images in your own mind's eye, so that you can live through the legends or the lives of the Gods. You do need to be able to see, whether from memory, or by pure imagination or by deliberately building an image from a written description. You will find that you can remember the faces and shapes of people you know well most easily if you actually sit down and work at recreating their picture with your eyes closed. This will come in very useful if you are trying to perform any absent healing, if you have been asked to do so. See a clear picture of the sick or injured person and then replace it with a new image of that person feeling healthy and full of energy. You can try the effect of this creative visualisation on yourself. If you are feeling under the weather or actually suffering from a particular infection, try seeing inside yourself. In the first instance imagine that, each time you breathe in, a golden aura of living light is sucked deep inside you, driving out despair and replacing it with energy and vitality. Breathe deeply and slowly at least twelve times, each time inhaling golden health and energy, and breathing out dark clouds of misery and depression. If you have a fever or a particular sickness, infection or tumour you should imagine a minute army of healing entities within you. See them massing at the site of the problem and carrying away heat, swelling or germs, destroying these and allowing them to be excreted from the body.

It may not be easy, especially if you are having orthodox medical treatment. Many of the drugs or intensive therapy have the unfortunate side-effect of making you feel tired and dispirited. Again, breathe deeply inhaling light and strength, and breathe out the murky feelings. Gradually you will begin to feel better, fevers will abate, and your strength to fight off the disease will increase. Many forms of alternative therapy actively encourage the idea of visualisation, of relaxing meditations, and inner journeys, when you see yourself in a place you enjoy, resting under a warm and healing sky, or being fit and sharing sport or other activity with your loved ones. It is worth making the effort to combat common colds, flu or any of the various virus infections which so often afflict people in the autumn and winter. Although you may be hot and weak, try to imagine a healing energy entering you, spreading through your veins, cooling your blood, bringing peaceful sleep, and continually increasing your strength every day.

Once you have experimented with these healing techniques and got them to work for yourself, you can guide others in the same methods, and be sure they will listen if you can assure them that imagining health returning will work. It is no alternative to receiving proper diagnosis and treatment, either orthodox or alternative, from fully trained practitioners and making every effort to follow their instructions for regular treatment. This is especially important if you have anything more serious than coughs and colds to deal with. You can certainly request the help of healing angels or gods and goddesses, especially if you ask them to show you the best cure for the problem. Leave time to listen to them! Meditate each day, quietly permitting new knowledge to seep through to you, no matter how strange it might seem. Your Holy Guardian Angel knows how best to help or heal you, and will explain suitable methods, given a chance.

You will also need to apply creative visualisation to the practice of ritual. By going through the whole event in your mind you can decide what equipment, symbols, regalia and furniture will be required. The things which you do not possess can be imagined during the actual ritual, but it is better to have real objects as far as possible. Certainly, adepts can imagine the entire rite, all the equipment, scents, scenery, music and personalities, but that is usually the result of having actually performed physical rites, with all the paraphernalia, frequently over many years. Practical experience ensures that the envisaged ceremony will be as powerful and effective as one in which a number of participants perform all the acts in person. The two sorts of events are not the same, however. The mental rite would go on within the performance of the actual ritual. The spoken invocations, physical gestures, the sharing of communion, and so on, all have their inner aspect, whereby the practitioners hold themselves in that controlled dual state of vision whereby they can perceive the inner planes and the outer room with all its symbolic equipment. As part of the ritual is performed for real, a duplicate activity is being carried out within the trained minds of all the participants, in a temple not built with hands, that is on a higher level of creation. Only much regular practice will lead to the smooth working of both levels in harmony, otherwise the experience is rather like being on a roller-coaster, and you seem to yoyo between several levels at once. Eventually you learn to hold the poised mental state so that the magically created scene is more real than the actual room. Obviously it is far easier to imagine clearly a scene which has been fully explained and described to you. To know what size, colour and shape every item is supposed to be, where it is and its inner function, makes this process easier. It is up to any decent lodge to instruct all its members in these details the — setting, tradition and symbolism of its temple. Often there is a lengthy pathworking designed specifically to do this at the start of every ritual, defining the Gods or Angelic Guardians, the symbolism of the Officers of the Quarters, and all other aspects of the work. Although this isn't usually a part of a witch's Opening the Circle, there is no reason why a pathworking setting the imaginary scene in a wild place rather than inside a house — as these rites are usually done — should not be shared by all.

If you are working alone then you will need to apply your imagination to the matter of myths. Every tradition has its hero tales, or legends of the Gods, and by reading these, and then following them in your vivid imagination they become real. You will find that by playing out any of the stories, whether or not you think them to be mere myths, you will get to recognise the great archetypal beings which turn up as Merlin, King Arthur, Guinevere, Morgan Le Fay and Galahad, for example. You will discover you can meet them, talk with them, share their adventures, and gradually understand what eternal principles they represent. The same is true of any legends or histories of the Gods. Read any books about them, look hard at the pictures of carvings or paintings, allowing the colours, shapes, symbols and garments to sink deeply into your consciousness. Take any figure and meditate upon every part of it, from the magical headdress to the sacred sandals. Learn from inner sources of instruction what each means, not merely to you, as a piece of information, but in terms of its true, cosmic meaning.

Using any kind of legendary material in this way, you can bring to life these ancient forces once again, to work with and learn from them. Study traditional ballads and poems, for much of our early magical history was only ever recorded in the lays of the bards, and yet some of these long and intertwined songs are still popular, and are found on folk-song LPs or in books of the words of ballads. Examine the journey of the hero to fairyland. Why does he have a milk-white steed? Why is the Queen of Faery dressed in green? Discover why the heroine was picking roses, and what colour they were, for each of these is a key to its inner and magical meaning. Every detail which these old songs have preserved had an important message. The same images turn up in dreams, bearing the same message, so it is in your own interest to study each story, look at its symbols in meditation, and visualise the characters and the plot, unfolding before your inner vision.

We have inherited a vast library of images, scenery and magical symbols which turn up in TV advertisements, in science fiction novels, in films and TV dramas. Not only are these adventures to be appreciated by us as the audience, but we can learn to participate. We can, in our own way, become the Grail Knight setting out on the Unfinished Quest, we can meet Herne the Hunter and fly with the Gabriel Hounds over the Western Land in storm and tempest, we can become the Queen of the Night or the Priestess of Isis if we learn to open the doors to that power. We can explore worlds of fact and fiction once we have learned to switch into alternative levels of existence, which most people would think of as mere fantasy. Magic teaches that they are real, that their doors can be gently opened and closed at will by anyone with the patience and skill to seek a way through. It is just another passage through the labyrinth which can be dis- covered and explored.

By learning to refocus our attention, relax our bodies yet awaken our minds, we have freedom to explore all levels of Creation. We can see our past lives by imagining ourselves travelling back through the corridors of time. By designing a simple pathworking wherein each of us walks slowly down a sloping passage, lined with doors to the ages past, we can arrive at a period in the history of the world where we may have lived and had our being before. By gently opening one door at a time we may peek through and see glimpses of the landscape, people and events at first from the outside, then if conditions feel right, by actually re-entering that time-zone. We can relive moments, both dull and exciting, re-experience love, hate and passion, retaste the food, smell it, perceive with our modern minds the clothing, transport, animals and buildings of a previous age in the same sort of finite reality which our everyday interaction with things around us does. It can be frightening, to turn up in the middle of a battle, and perhaps suffer wounds or death, to be involved in the daily grind of the world's peasants, to be hungry and cold and wet and find ourselves in smelly and draughty hovels as most people lived during many of their lives. We may be slaves or serfs, sick or maimed, suffering continuous child-bearing, miscarriages, rape or death in childbirth. We may reawaken as tormented children, dying before we have really lived at all. Look hard at history and you will see that 75 per cent of people were servants, landless, downtrodden, poor and hungry at any period in time and any place in the world. You are unlikely to have missed your share of misery, plague, wars and starvation. No one really was always a priestess or queen, a person of wealth and power in every life – only in fiction!

You can apply the same mental art of controlled relaxation and mental refocusing to astral travel. By working hard at gaining separation of either your consciousness or your actual astral body from the rest of you, you can visit places at a distance, to gain knowledge and information. True astral travel requires very special conditions, total lack of disturbance, or, safest of all, a considerate companion who will watch over you, asking questions, if appropriate, or helping you to make an exit to other worlds. Take care: the results can be disturbing or frightening. It may seem to be fun to be separated from your body, and be able to float through walls and over roofs, but it is an enormous shock when it actually starts to happen. You may even find yourself hovering near the ceiling of your room, looking down on your own body, and that gives you such a shock that you shoot back into your relaxed self with such force that it gives you palpitations and a cold sweat. Otherwise you can just drift off, losing awareness of time and distance, and lose yourself in the vastness of space, and only return later, feeling physically cold and stiff, and sometimes utterly exhausted. It really is much safer to try mere projection of consciousness, where your divided perception does allow you to be aware of any discomfort in your body, before it becomes critical, and will bring you back gently and totally into normal awareness. Projection of consciousness has the added advantage that you can communicate with your companion, answer questions, draw pictures, describe what you can see and experience, in real time, as it happens.

Don't play with these advanced states of consciousness until you really can meditate at the drop of a hat, anywhere and at any time. You need to have confidence in being able to relax fully into your bodiless self but to be able to return quickly, gently and fully at will. You need to know where you are intending to go, for how long, and definitely not to meddle in the lives or affairs of other people. You may go back through time, either by the Corridor of the Ages, or by visiting the Akashic Records, which are frequently encountered as a vast library, filled with ancient volumes on seemingly endless shelves. Modern seekers have seen hi-tech areas too, with microchip equipment, video screens and electronic consoles instead of, or as well as, the rows and rows of books. Somewhere in that vast store is the Book of your Life or Lives. You have a right to examine it, and can ask to be guided to it. It may seem huge and ancient, or it could be one of the modern microfiche versions, you never can tell until you seek it out. In the book you may discover scenes and landscapes which awaken such feelings of longing, such uncomfortable sensations and pressures of long-forgotten relationships that you are made to weep, or laugh or dance for joy. The inner memories have enormous power, especially in the area of emotions and deep-seated feelings which are not usually easy to control or quell either, once they are evoked back into your living memory.

Once you begin to explore these regions within, take your time. It can have strange side-effects on your dreams and meditations which get much worse if you plunge into hours of exploration every day. Do use common sense and only take a new trip when you have fully understood everything that the last one brought to the surface. Because much of what you learn from inner mental sources has no obvious mundane equivalent it is not usually something you can discuss with those around you. They might think you are mad, they might also actually begin to take steps to have your mental health investigated if you insist on discussing the latest revelation, or your conversation with the Archangel Gabriel, or the notion that you were Cleopatra in your last life. Most people take these kinds of matters with a pinch of salt, and you can quickly lose your credibility if you insist that your vision is true. It may well be, but discretion and silence are safer by far. Again, it is a good reason to discover magical companions of one sort or another, for at least then you can compare notes and share experiences which to the ordinary person appear to be the workings of a diseased mind.

Your religious revelations, too, should be treated with a certain amount of confidentiality. Religious nuts are the worst sort, and anyone who goes round preaching some far-fetched cosmic truth will meet with a good deal of opposition. You may indeed acquire privileged information or some kind of direct message from God, but it doesn't give you the automatic right to shout it from the housetops and expect to be believed. New directions of philosophy and religious thought are emerging at this time at the end of

the Piscean Age, but the message will need to be fully understood
before it is laid before the general public. It is possible that some
genuine guidance and direction is being brought through, by
meditation, by revelation and by messages from Inner Plane
Adepti, but it will need assessment and refinement before it can
be spread about as the Gospel of the New Age.

You will always know what is right, what ought to be thoroughly mulled over, and what should be acted upon instantly if
you allow yourself a few sessions of meditation to discover the
answers. You will find, if you take care, that each step in your
magical progress will always be the right one for you at that
moment, if you resist the desire to know all, to experience all
before you are really ready. Patience is indeed a virtue, one of the
most important to modern occultists. At every step there will be
choices, but you will certainly make the best one if you listen to
your inner self, or allow time and tide to dictate the next stage of
your progress. This may not be as exciting as getting a new book,
turning to the advanced exercises at the end, without thoroughly
reading and understanding the entire text first, and so failing to
get any benefit from your impatience.

Tread warily, especially if you are making these strange inner
voyages alone. There is no intrinsic harm in occult knowledge,
the practice of ritual magic, or pursuit of wisdom from the Ages,
but there is ample opportunity for self-deception, straying from
the path of common sense into the mire of confusion and doubt. It
is easy to claim great powers, degrees and knowledge, which is a
false front, put on to impress those who are sillier than you, for
the true light will shine hard through such a facade, and you will
soon be shown up as a fraud. Act with humility, for you will be
dealing with mighty forces. These are, on the whole, on the side
of cosmos against chaos, but destruction and decay are just as
much parts of evolution as are growth and expansion. It won't
feel like that when some long-held ideal crumbles into dust,
because its time is ended. It won't help if you cling to the shattered
remains, doing your best to hold them together, as that will prove
to be a waste of energy. It sometimes is necessary to accept the
changes of decay just as you must accept the changes of growth,
which can cause you to become too big for your comfortable
situations, which like old clothes, will become too tight and
eventually split. Like a butterfly emerging from a chrysalis, you
will come forth greater and able to travel through more realms,

but getting out of the hard shell may be a painful and unpleasant process while it is actually happening.

Within you is the potential for much good, for much growth and much love and joy. Each of these will be given to you as rewards as you travel your road through life. Although you may seem to back-track, to get lost in dead-ends, to wander from the straight and narrow path and get lost in desires, and even though illusions of power and the darkness of ignorance may temporarily overwhelm you, in the end you will reach your own personal goal. By becoming aware of the levels of your inner self, your Holy Guardian Angel or anima/mus, or whatever term you prefer, you will gain a great ally, who will go with you wherever you might wander, encouraging, guiding, inspiring and fulfilling your needs. Learn to become aware of that source of help, open up those doors and permit it to guide your spirit through the inner lands. No one can do this for you. Only you can feed your spiritual self, explore its realms, gain insights and power from the wisdom which comes from practical experience. The way towards these invisible goals is always in front of you, but you have to make the personal commitment and dedication to seek it out.

In essence, that is what initiation is all about. It means 'I Go In', a lonely and personal entry, even at the hands of experienced teachers and companions. Your experiences at that moment will leave a deep impression on you, but it will be a meaningless sham unless you understand what is supposed to happen. It is not just the drama of the death and rebirth, but a spiritual rebirth, the taking on of a new life, which is what matters.

CHAPTER NINE

Short-Cuts to Power

Here they are no longer talking of what is Good and Evil, or of
what is Right or Wrong, and puzzling themselves in Satan's labyrinth,
But are conversing with Eternal Realities as they Exist in the Human
Imagination.

William Blake on THE VISION OF THE LAST JUDGEMENT

Today, when the media bombards us with information and
advertisements for all kinds of goods and services, the magical
world has not escaped this influx of opportunists and people in
search of a fast buck. Many of those who are seeking information, instruction or help are in a vulnerable state of mind.
Either because they are confused or worried about their lives or
health, they accept the glossy brochures, the expansive offers of
instant power, and the 'Change your Luck with a Magic Pixie'
charms, sold by the thousand, because they have no criteria to
judge these claims, for they are in a new area of knowledge. Of
course some of the millions of people who do buy some 'magical
object' will have better luck, health or win the pools, and will
write in showing their delight, but thousands of the others get no
change, or, sometimes life gets even worse.

We are all gullible to some extent. If we were not, advertising simply wouldn't work. The offers of cheap prices, low interest, quick service or angelic assistance will all attract some of us to venture into buying whatever is on offer. It might be a bar of chocolate, or it might be a system of magical training, a 'spell kit' or an infallible talisman to solve all life's little worries overnight. Certainly each of us has to choose what we will fall for, accepting that a chocolate bar won't kill us, and that the information pack offered by the Magical School could be exactly what we require, but credulity should run out when it comes to the 'infallible spell' simply because nothing in life is that certain. If, for example, we enter a coupon for the weekly football pools we don't expect every entry to be a winner. We might be lucky and scoop a prize, but more often than not, we win nothing. Those who advertise charms and talismans which will help everyone are implying that every entry into the competition will win a valuable prize. Do you believe that?

What it is really important to do, if you require outside help, is to read any announcement about services or any kind of magical talisman very carefully. Some will say 'individually crafted, send details of birthplace and date' as well as the problem you want solved, which does imply that the maker will in some way attune the finished product to the individual who requested it. Of course you have no guarantee that this will happen, and you might be sent a plastic, mass-produced item of no magical power! That is always the risk you take. A further factor is that being made by someone other than yourself it won't be directly linked to you and your troubles, unless you actually have to dedicate the talisman when it is received, and carry out a 'turning on' act of some sort. When you make any sort of talisman for yourself it will be many times more powerful, simply because, fumbling though your efforts might be, the thing is created by you with sincerity and need.

The study and practice of magic is always a 'chicken and egg' sort of situation. Which should come first? Do you try to learn some of the basic arts on your own so that your discrimination and powers of perception are awoken and attuned, or do you plunge into joining the first coven in your area which offers initiation next week? There isn't a simple answer for we are all different and our individual needs vary from time to time. It certainly does help if you have a basic understanding of yourself, which should be arrived at by honest, secret self-inspection. This ought to be an ongoing process, for the more you really know about yourself the more real information you have about other people, and through them, the universe at large. You will have to decide if the commitment you are willing to make at this moment is geared more towards a group of other people, or inwards towards your own potential for wisdom.

There is no substitute for hard work, whether with a group or on your own. Eventually, if you take magic seriously, you will have to learn something about the Gods, about the Elements, about the Seasonal Festivals, your relationships with people, and much, more more. This information and practical experience cannot be built up in a few weeks, or mysteriously granted to you because of a rite of initiation in the hands of the Supreme Master of the Whole Universe, or whatever! As you learn more about yourself, you will become more aware of what you wish to do next, and your perceptions about offers of group membership, or of the value of training exercises for yourself will become clearer. The more you know about magic in general, and your own objectives, the easier each choice will become. So long as you always apply common sense, you are unlikely to stray too far from the shortest path of inner progress, for you will be guided if you are willing to listen to your Holy Guardian Angel or Inner Guide, who speaks – when he can get a word in edgeways. Learn to be still, and the path will made clearer.

Most novices face a wide variety of options – whether to become a well-publicised sort of witch, or take up the less well-known way of the ceremonial magician, or the even less well-defined path of the solo shaman. There are, in fact, many other options for following various traditions, like the Egyptian, Greek, Celtic or Red Indian, not to mention Atlantean, Extra-terrestrial or any other path towards true knowledge. There are developments like those pioneered by Aleister Crowley (who always spelled magick with a 'k' to distinguish it from conjuring and stage magic) and the even more recent concept of Chaos Magick, in which you do what you like, and suffer the conse-quences of your actions when karma catches up with you! You can follow the Right-Hand Path of white or evolutionary magic, or take the Left-Hand Path of black or destructive magic. You can commit yourself to any of the contacted schools of instruction, involving at least four years of practical and mental training before initiation may be offered, or you can take the loneliest option, that which leads towards solo study and perhaps self-initiation.

Many people imagine that initiation is a first step towards occult expertise, but in fact, it is quite an advanced one, for it is really a recognition of knowledge already gained, and the candidate's readiness to be admitted to the work of the lodge or coven. To be fully admitted into any sort of esoteric group requires a lot of ongoing commitment. Occasionally people come to Britain from overseas, for example, and expect to be admitted to a coven, in particular, because it is closer to the roots of the Gardnerian Tradition, or some other branch of the Old Religion. They then expect to be able to return to their own land and pass on that initiation. This is very seldom a real possibility because having joined any group you will be expected to work with it for a long time. You are never bound for life, except to unprincipled groups who have no right to admit people in the first place, so be careful if you have to swear an oath. Any decent group will allow you to resign from it 'in good standing' if personal commitments, a move of home or job, or family needs make your outside work require priority. You may be permitted, after further training, to rejoin, if you so wish, but don't count on it. People who go around joining all sorts of different groups, whether at the same time, or one after another, without really allowing the training or tradition of any of them to teach the wandering seeker anything, are wasting their time, as well as the scarce resources of the groups they 'visit' so briefly. Such behaviour is frowned upon, so give any group you join at least a year, to discover if it really is for you, or not.

Do take care, if you answer an advertisement to join any sort of order or society, that you have a fair idea of the kind of people who already belong, what their aims and objectives are, and what you will be expected to offer in return for membership. Any worthwhile group will be happy to explain its philosophy, introduce you to other members, and answer general questions about its aims and methods. The best sorts of orders will have Outer Courts, open meetings, which offer basic instruction, or regular lectures to anyone, so that possible candidates have a clear idea what that society's objectives are. Others run postal or occasional one-day training courses, again to give a novice a solid grounding in the inner group's philosophy and practices. Any occult order, especially if it has a rather dramatic title, which will not give straightforward answers to any queries you may have, or which is evasive, or generally unhelpful, should be left alone until you are sure you have enough personal knowledge to be able to cope with joining it.

Most of the really nasty groups, which thankfully in Britain are quite few in number, 'feel' distinctly weird, and the kind of questions they might ask potential members will indicate they are not all they might be. Any organisation which enquires first about your income and your sexual activities, or seems to prefer very young, that is teenage, members (some good groups won't accept students under 25!), or have free ideas about the use of drugs, bondage or domination should cause Seekers to be very wary. There is a genuine magical police force in operation and this will act, on the Inner Planes, to sort out the truly nasty peoȷ e, but there has always been a kind of grey area, luring members in with promises of all kinds of power and goodies, which can lead not to esoteric enlightenment, but to drug addiction, AIDS through careless sex, mental disturbance and possibly gaol or death. If you encounter any such organisation in your search for occult wisdom, do have the sense to report your suspicions to any of the well-established occult magazines, for they have links with those who can investigate, on several levels, and discover if your worries are true.

The various New Age philosophies which are taught in some Western as well as some Eastern traditions may include ideas which are strange to you. Crowley's well-publicised 'Do as thou wilt shall be the whole of the Law, Love is the Law, Love under Will' was not new to him, and those who understand its inner meaning do not accept it as free licence to do what they like. His works are very much concerned with learning what your True Will is, and even a moment's casual thought will show that what is meant is not merely 'Do what you like ...' The oldest magical adage, written above the door of the Temple of Eleusis can be translated as 'Know Yourself'. Self-knowledge is the first step towards knowing anything else in magic. You can only discover your true will by seeing what part of you actually wills it, and by finding out your ambitions and desires. Unless you really want to tread the Left-Hand Path of Selfishness, for which you will inevitably pay, probably threefold, you cannot use your magic to please yourself.

It might sound fun to be able to influence the love of your life into a lifelong dedication, but he or she has free will, and any kind of magic which binds others to you is part of the Dark Road to self-destruction. There are lots of books which offer love spells, and show you how to make love potions, but anything which compels another into any situation, be it a relationship, or a state of good or bad health is destructive magic. Try to understand what it might be like to be on the receiving end of such a spell, some of which will have a serious effect upon the recipient. You would not be able to make any new relationships but would be forced to think only about the person who performed the spell. You would become a sort of zombie with only one thought, underneath which your own will, which might be aimed at someone else, or a freer situation, would be repressed and frustrated. Your waking life would be very uncomfortable because you would be obsessed with the spell-maker, and most likely your dreams would be full of unpleasant images too. That is the effect of following the Left-Hand Path. It leads to destruction of the self, so that the spell-maker ends up with only a shell of the person he desired, not their true self. Love has to be earned. First you must learn to see your own true worth and develop self-love. Then you must learn to love your neighbour, who, in the biblical sense, is anyone you come upon in your daily life. It is through your ability to give out love that you earn some for yourself. If you desire someone, then make yourself the object of their desire. Become their ideal lover, changing yourself to suit their wishes, not impelling their unsought love for you.

As well as self-knowledge you need to have self-respect. It is customary for those who are being trained in Western ceremonial magic to spend several moments each day in focused self-awareness. In earlier times it was usual to greet the sunrise each day, affirming your wish to serve the Lord of Light. At noon it was a time to ask for a blessing and briefly link in with all the other followers of that path, and on retiring it is a good idea to work through the day, resolving any difficulties, planning for the morrow, and tying up loose ends. Last thing it is always wise to say a prayer of thanks for any benefits gained during the day. Like meditation realisations, these moments may not individually be vastly important, but they add structure to your day, and there is a cumulative benefit to be gained from acknowledging inner links regularly. This self-imposed discipline does help you to get used to meditating and being in contact with the more subtle aspects of yourself. Some Orders will expect their members to keep a detailed diary showing that these daily observances are kept, or whatever the reason might be that some have been forgotten or missed. It may seem very hard, having to greet the sun, perform a meditation and perhaps some exercises in visualisation, symbolism and occult study every day, or at least five days a week, to record in a book your realisations, dreams, details of books you have read or other things you have learned, and then look through your achievements when you go to bed, but it does pay dividends. Regular practice of sport is necessary to advance your standard, rehearsal of words and actions of a play, regular sessions with your instrument increase your musical ability, just as speaking a foreign language as much as possible increases your fluency. Practical magic requires at least as much dedication as any or even all of these!

One of the other exercises which is recommended to some beginners which needs further knowledge to get the best results is that of performing 'Banishing Rituals'. Many books, both ancient and modern suggest that on retiring at night, or before a ritual, meditation or any divination a Cleansing Rite is performed, which drives out any conflicting influences. What these erudite sources forget is that such rituals need to be removed at the end of the time they are required for, and that the banishing should be revoked. Otherwise, because they work by sweeping away all sorts of psychic energies and distractions, they can also sweep away contact with other human company, they can drive out friendship, and create a sphere of cold emptiness around the novice. This sense of abandonment and the awakened senses can be reasons why a newcomer can feel he is under psychic attack. He isn't, but because the normal clatter of psychic information, which we are just aware of, has been silenced, and because his ability to sense his own body and any energies which surround him is increased, there might be a feeling of foreboding. There are seldom any really uncomfortable energies which have to be banished before meditation or going to bed, unless you live in a very unhappy environment. Even then, the banishing should be ended when you complete the work, or first thing in the morning. A banishing does work, and will drive out all influences, good and bad, so use these ceremonies with care.

There are occasional reasons for exorcism, which like many occult arts, is something only to be attempted after many years' study and practice. People can attract bad energies to them, but this is very rare and over ninety per cent of what people imagine to be 'psychic attacks' come from inside themselves. Magical training, or careless dabbling with ouija boards or seances, without any kind of proper spiritual guidance, can awaken hidden depths of your character, and some of them are dark and murky, for they are aspects of your self which you have repressed. The Light of Wisdom will shine on everything, good and bad, and the dingy facets show up worst. You cannot banish these, and the harder you try, the more dense and unpleasant they may become. Getting a heavyweight exorcist in to try to budge these parts of you which are just as real as your left arm can do far more harm than good. It is for this reason that the magical exorcist is one of the most advanced and experienced members of his Order, for as well as being a well-controlled psychic, so that he can see what is really going on, he needs the wisdom to counsel those who are haunted by their own nature. It is certainly not a matter of rushing in with bell, book and candle, especially if you haven't actually read the book, and don't have a match to light the candle! If you feel in need of exorcism then seek out expert help. The chances are you need information and guidance more than a bath in Holy Water.

You will have to make up your own mind about ghosts. There is plenty of well-documented evidence for their frequent sighting, there are photographs, films and tape-recorded noises. As your inner senses develop, you will certainly become very aware of atmospheres in houses, ancient and modern, and of the lingering emotions trapped in old walls, on battlefields, in hospitals and churches. You may be able to see things which aren't there, as far as the rest of the population is concerned, like flying saucers and their occupants, ghosts, or tree dryads (those vast multi-legged beings who take care of all our woodlands, and can be encountered by the Wise, and asked for help). You will discover that museums contain a lot more than dead mummy cases and old jewellery, and that library books retain traces of some of the people who have read them. If you attune this particular ability you will be able to 'psychometrise' objects, and read from them their history, and details of the lives of their owners. You will find that you can understand what is troubling a sick person, and perhaps the seat of their illness, so that you can shine your healing power upon that place.

Poltergeists are another matter. These seem always to be associated with young people, usually approaching puberty, or going through some kind of mental turmoil. Although heavy furniture and bricks may be tossed about by the energies which can be produced under rare circumstances at this time of life, people are seldom harmed by this wild and frightening turn of events. They cannot really be exorcised, because, like other sorts of personal hauntings, they are part of the young person at the centre of the stage. That is often the reason for their occurrence. A growing youngster, entering a crucial time in his or her life, when internal chemical changes are having strange effects on both body and mind, desperately needs love and reassurance. If this is denied, or overlooked, then the energies build up and explode, causing objects to fly about, and the child, driven by forces he cannot comprehend, may unconsciously do all kinds of strange things, like writing on walls, and because he may seem to have superhuman strength, breaking things he could hardly be expected even to lift. Again, counselling is the answer. Pay heed to the teenager, find time to allow him to talk, make sure he gets plenty of outdoor exercise or sport, and restful sleep at night. Allow the young person to understand the responsibilities of growing up, yet do not thrust these youngsters – however adult they may seem – into roles beyond their years. The joys and fun of childhood can never be replaced. It is the simplicity of vision and directness found in all young children that the adult magician strives to recover. The ability to see clearly and judge character, to be able to 'imagine' things, so often used as a condemnation when someone's mind is extra creative, to be able to accept that you can fly, and do all the things that cartoon heroes can do, these are what grown-up occultists struggle very hard to rediscover in themselves. So if you have to deal with poltergeist phenomena, bear this in mind. Help the child gently to emerge from the freedom of youth caringly into the heavy responsibility and natural limitations of growing up. It isn't a time to do anything except call upon his own Holy Guardian Angel to take the youngster under its wings, protect and guide him until he can cope with life in his new role. Heavy exorcisms will only engrain peculiar behaviour into the child, and it will be hard to outgrow it.

There are ways of magically dealing with really nasty haunts, those found at the sites of murders, or severe accidents, nuclear disasters and old battles, but these are best not tackled by anyone with less than seven years' experience in magical work. If you do encounter somewhere where the place feels unpleasant, simply call upon the Light to cleanse it and control it. This will alert those on the Inner Planes who deal with such matters and help will arrive, visible or otherwise, in due course. There are plenty of beneficial spirits, angels or saints hovering around who will gladly take over tasks beyond any magical novice's powers, if they are politely requested to assist. Often, if you visit the place again later it will feel better.

As your studies progress you will need to consider your own feelings about good and evil, which in esoteric paths are usually looked upon as Light and Dark, which do not have the same weighted implications. Night and day, summer and winter, left and right, up and down, all are natural pairs, neither being dominant over the other. That is the main objective of following the Middle Way, a road of total balance, both within and without, physical and spiritual. It isn't easy, but I expect that by now you have realised that anything worth doing isn't easy, either! This has been referred to as the Bridge of the Sword Blade, or the Knife Edge, and turns up in the Arthurian Legends. The path to the Light has always been narrow, crossing the Abyss by a slender and shaking rainbow bridge, built only of your will to cross. Below is what you have evolved from, the cast-off skins of your previous beings, and on your back, like the Fool in the Tarot deck, is a satchel with all the good you may achieve, hung from your wand and bound with the cord of your intentions. As you wander the maze paths of life you will encounter those to whom you have to give something from your pack, and in other situations you will learn lessons, or gain magical prizes which can be stored within your satchel. You will always have the choice of when and what to give, but the better you understand your own nature the clearer such choices will become.

In universal terms, and those of physics, Darkness is an absence of Light. Darkness is not a thing which overcomes Light: it has no substance, nor dimension, nor power, except that, in inner terms, it may gain power we invest it with. If you encounter people who offer you riches or worldly goods, domination over others and all the kinds of desirable options which fiction talks of, you will have to choose. Eventually, willing or not, you will need to pay for what you take. It might not cost you an arm and a leg, it might cost you your chance of evolution! The esoteric philosophies teach of balance as the key factor. Dark seeks to outweigh Light, yet Light seeks only balance, harmony, peace. There is a difference. When the forces of Light are called into battle they will restore the essential pattern of day and night; they do not strive to wipe out night, or winter, or decay, or rest, but to allow them to take their proper place in Creation, it is for this reason that there are goddesses as well as gods, and those goddesses have a dark, decaying and seemingly destructive side to their characters. This is the natural decay of things which have outgrown their time, and this dissolution is as important as growth. Think what the world would be like if nothing rotted back into the earth – dead leaves, dead people, excrement piled over the whole world, and the world starving for lack of nourishment.

Destruction is a force of change, whereas the chaotic powers of those who follow the Dark Road seek to halt evolution, which is also change, so that the whole world goes into a static state. Nothing will grow, or give birth, or die, or decay. There are many legends about evil wizards who lay curses to that effect upon the land, and it is the Knight in Shining Armour who seeks to restore the alternating power of life and death. Death itself is only a stage in the long and winding path through the labyrinth of experience. Death leads to rebirth, and the endless natural cycles of Creation continue in their harmonious patterns. Be willing to face the changes in your life, and outgrow the desire to have everything, to halt the progress from one experience to the next. There may be alluring offers of magical powers, success and riches, but do look hard at those who make such offers! Do they look like the kind of people you might wish to become? Do their eyes shine with health and love of life? Are they pleasant and unassuming? Or do they demand things of you that you would rather not give? Yours is the choice, and in the end you will have to pay the price in full.

Much of what appears of the occult path to the outside world is illusion. Occult means 'hidden, obscured' and it really is like that. Those who become Insiders have a totally different outlook to those who can only gaze in longingly, and speculate as to what does go on in the witches' circles, in the closed lodges of the High Magicians, in the Shaman's cave or the Wise Old Woman's cottage in the woods. There may well come a time when you will need to take your courage in both hands and ask to be admitted. Some groups expect you to ask to come in, others will invite you. Often there is an element of both, for you must show willing by preparing yourself as well as you can for admission to coven or lodge, by learning thoroughly whatever is taught to you, and by seizing all opportunities to know more. You may ask to be permitted to take the irrevocable step of initiation, but you must also prove you have the patience to wait, and not abandon a reasonable chance of becoming an Insider with a reputable, if cautious, society by hastily joining some fly-by-night group which offers you immediate initiation for a fat fee and a bottle of red wine!

Magic does look exciting from the outside, and it is, but only because trained initiates know how to enter safely those levels where adventure, knowledge, beauty and truth abound. They do it mainly by sitting still, in a quiet room with their eyes closed, having grown out of the need to leap about, waving swords, whilst dressed in fabulous robes. There are occasions when 'fancy dress' and elaborate rituals are necessary, and for most magical orders these form a fair part of their activities, but it is what is actually going on in the heads of the participants which really matters, and that may be altogether different.

There are short-cuts to power and wealth, people who follow them fill the gaols, as con-men, embezzlers, drug-dealers and thieves. If that is your aim in life, no doubt there is some way you can set off on that dark road without the hard work of mastering magic.

Some people approach various aspects of occult study as ways to make money, and think, that after reading a book or two, they can set up as astrologers, Tarot readers or rune experts, and charge fat fees in the hopes that their clients will know even less about the subject than they do! To master the arts of divination takes many years of practical work, firstly in knowing the symbolism of the system thoroughly, knowing how the method evolved, how it can be applied and what it can tell you about a person, the future or the way problems may be solved. This wisdom cannot be gained from a book. Nor can it be readily known by a young person: you need to have lived in the world for at least twenty-five or thirty years before you have experienced enough of life to be able to understand other people, and hopefully, yourself too. Giving parrot-like readings is foolish, and it is also against the very strict ethics by which all divinatory arts are ruled. The charging of money for any kind of magical work is really against the rules. Certainly, if someone requires you to make a solid-gold talisman, studded with emeralds, at a certain aspect of the moon's cycle, when particular planets are well-aspected, you have every right to ask them to obtain the gold, have the emeralds cut to the proper sizes, but you cannot honestly ask for payment for making the talisman or blessing it.

Sadly festivals and exhibitions do not help. They charge quite high rents for spaces so that diviners have to exact a fee from clients, yet what they get is a very inferior reading! No one, not even the world's most talented psychic, really likes trying to read cards in a public place, with strangers, and their myriad energies flooding all over the place, and distracting sounds, smells and the press of people nudging the table and making odd comments as they try to focus on the client and his problems. It is always best to examine any such readers and discover one you feel in harmony with and then *make a private appointment* so you get their full attention, and allow their inner sight to give an in-depth interpretation of whatever their divinatory system happens to be. Everyone will gain, you will get true wisdom, and may make a friend, and the reader will be totally attentive to all the subtle nuances of the reading, giving clarity and depth to it.

It is true that you have to pay for courses of instruction. Sometimes this is because they are residential, and bed and board cost money. Many of the locations where esoteric courses are run, over weekends or during the week, are themselves controlled by organisations with an unusual philosophy, or links with meditation or alternate therapy, so they accept that people need to have quiet for inner journeys, or are not alarmed when a class turns up for some sessions in robes and sandals, instead of jeans and tee-shirts. The courses run at hotels tend not to be so free, and the robe-wearing and incense-burning is a bit limited, and so are the practical sessions. Tutors often have to come from far away and so need their travel expenses paid, although on the whole occult teachers don't expect vast fees for giving a course of instruction.

Other courses may have to have books or lesson papers printed, cassette tapes of exercises recorded and duplicated, usually by the 'real-time' system which cuts down on background noise and distortion, which can be so distracting when you are listening quietly to the pathworking. Postage, administration, advertising, printing information brochures for all the people who don't take up the course – all these things cost money which ultimately has to be recovered from those who accept the training. Some tutors have ordinary jobs and have to fit their magic lectures and divination training into spare time, others are writers or researchers who may devote their entire energies to teaching and working in the esoteric field, but who do not make huge salaries like people in the materialistic world.

Where novices do need to exercise caution is when obviously

commercial enterprises are offering 'Ritual Kits', 'Instantly Effective Talismans' and 'Immediate Power Courses'. They have to judge whether the kind of people running shops and businesses are going to have sufficient time to develop themselves to the point that their offerings are going to really work. As has been said all along, unless you aim to perfect the person you are, developing your inner self, then what you do in the world may be useless. The Inner Way goes in the opposite direction to the path of the materialistic world; the treasures you aim to build up are in 'heaven', or some subtle interior place. Wealth, power, position in the outer world have no meaning, nor does any art which leaves the spirit untended and hungry. Feed the soul, control the will, and all those things which in eternal terms are worth seeking may be yours. You cannot buy them with gold, sacrifice anything to obtain them, or be given them by any external agency, no matter what their advertisements may suggest. You have to work on yourself and earn them and they will be paid freely and in full value by those Guardians of the Mysteries in whose hands all the inner treasures of the universe lie as gifts.

Be willing to ask questions of anyone involved in any society or a supplier of equipment. Your own judgement is very important. If things don't feel right, give them a miss. A better option will appear – be certain of that. If you require a divination find out how long the reader has been studying, try to meet previous clients and get their views of what they were told. No decent Tarot reader will mind because she will know what you are told would be complimentary. Don't accept guidance or advice which goes against your own feelings. The latest craze, spreading in from America, is 'channelling', a form of mediumship or mediation whereby invisible entities pass on information or advice through the agency of a human individual. Some of this may well be genuine and sound, coming directly from some angelic source, correctly passed on by the channeller; a lot of it may be pure rubbish, flooding out from the disturbed psyche of an untrained and uncontrolled subconsciousness. You will simply have to decide for yourself. Again, ask how long a person has been doing this sort of thing, have they had any kind of training, do they know about self-protection and what guarantees are there that what they say comes from anywhere but themselves? A genuine mediator will be happy to answer such questions and explain their qualifications and experience.

It used to be written that to expand your magical knowledge it would be necessary 'to buy an egg without haggling ...' and in some cases that still holds good, for you will intuitively recognise what is the true value of something worth having, be it seemingly cheap or dear, but there are other instances, if your own financial circumstances are not too healthy (there are no rich witches!) in which you can barter. Offer other forms of payment than cash, if there is something you know you require, be it training, equipment, advice or some other commodity. Offer your time or some skill to make something to exchange for what you need. This will often be acceptable, and the gentle links forged in such a way may stand you in good stead in the future.

The material path – that which leads to owning things, to domination of your own spirit, not the wisdom to set it free, the desire to possess other people, to envy their position, to covet their friends, to be jealous of another's looks or lifestyle – can never run in the same direction as the spiritual way. It is not necessary to give away all your possessions and live in a cave, owning nothing and relying on the birds for food, but you may have to give up the *desire* to possess things, to own the latest design, the most fashionable clothes, today's material bargain. Once you have learned to cast off the heavy burden of ownership and excessive lusting after objects and people, you will be free to share in the limitless and freely given bounty of the entire spiritual world. You may have stewardship of a nice house, win the love of a beautiful partner, gain respect and honour because you have earned them, and discover you have access to all the riches of your inner being, to your complete capacity to make use of them. You will own little, learn to live simply, delight in the beauty of ever-changing nature, rather than have a valuable masterpiece hanging on your wall. Every day will bring you greater fulfilment, further delight and endless rewards for the efforts you have put into recognising what are the real treasures. Just don't be too ready to be taken in by the promises others make, especially those in advertisements, unless you can check very thoroughly what is on offer, if it is what you need, and if it can be had at a price you can afford to part with. Not only could the price be a matter of money, it could be your own integrity and ethical position. Nothing is worth sacrificing your good name and conscience for, and those things you really require will never cost more than you can afford, in eternal terms.

CHAPTER TEN

The Way Out – Back to the World

> He may by contemplation learn
> A little more than what he knew,
> And even see great oaks return
> To acorns out of which they grew.
>
> He may, if he but listen well,
> Through twilight and the silence here
> Be told what there are none may tell,
> To vanity's impatient ear;
>
> And he may never dare again
> Say what awaits him, or be sure
> What sunlit labyrinth of pain
> He may not enter and endure.
>
> Who knows today from yesterday
> May learn to count no thing too strange,
> Love builds of what Time takes away,
> Till Death itself is less than Change.

Edwin Arlington Robinson, 'HILLCREST'

There may come a time (it may already have happened to you, while you have been reading this book) that you recognise that the Occult Path, the Inner Way, the Road to Initiation is not the one for you. It isn't everyone's choice, for the pleasures of the world, the commitments to home, family or job can take precedence, but if you have made any steps on the Hidden Way there are things you should do before you will be free of it, and its responsibilities.

If you have joined a group or groups and now feel ready to depart then you must recognise that such parting needs to be formal. You can't, in magic, just wander off to pastures new, leaving behind links with previous commitments and associations. Every order or coven, no matter how loosely knit or well-established,has an *aegis*, a shadow on a mental plane which will lie over you until you actually request its withdrawal. You may need to write a letter of resignation to the group which admitted you, or to make the secret severing ritual from the gods you chose to worship in private. If you made commitments formally, or through initiation, then you have to unmake them, just as you must banish the circle at the conclusion of the rite. Simply disappearing from the human group will not be enough. Those links are forged on the inner, and they will endure through time, through distance, and even through lives to come, so unless you free yourself of the shackles which you freely took up, you will remain bound.

Although it is on a lesser level, even the connections with occult journals which you now wish to stop receiving can leave traces which will affect you, until you have the common decency, or the courtesy, to write and explain why you no longer wish to subscribe. Even if it is mundane poverty rather than a difference of philosophy which causes the separation, this should be explained, not only to get yourself off their mailing list (many of which nowadays are computerised, and occasionally shared with other more persistent organisations) but to free yourself from any lingering associations made on the inner. A brief but polite letter will have the correct effect, and you will be disentangled from anything which could bother you later on.

Another situation which might arise, though in practice it is fairly rare, is when you are cast out of a group or coven for breaking their rules. Often there are power struggles within new groups and factions divide off and folk who strive to hold a middle ground can end up cast out of both sections. You might, on the other hand, be a member of an order which is expelling someone, and have to watch the process from the inside. It doesn't happen very often and in ritual magical lodges, at least, is looked upon as a very serious step. The most common reasons are when someone has broken their oath of secrecy, or who has not attended meetings, or has openly quarrelled with senior members of the organisation. Usually the recreant is carefully counselled about his behaviour, and given warnings, but if these are ignored, he might find himself being dislodged.

If you do swear an oath it is a serious undertaking. You are giving your word to behave in a particular way, to exercise discretion in what you say about the organisation and its members in open company, and how you interact with them. If you are requested to perform certain exercises and you don't do them, without a good reason, or if you brag about your initiation, give away passwords or symbols which are sacred to that group, you are asking for trouble. Words are power in magic. Look at the Bible: 'In the beginning was the Word ...' Your word is indeed your bond, and, like it or not, you have promised something, so you must keep to that, or at least request to do something different. It is true that many oaths published in books based on nineteenth-century orders may have bloodthirsty penalties for oath-breakers, but if you actually look at the wording it generally says something like 'It would *be better that* my throat should be cut *than I break my given word.*' Not 'If I break my word, it *will* happen!' The Inner Plane Adepti have very subtle and powerful ways of exacting penance from those who renege on their promises. If you have to pay for some misdemeanour, the price will not be what you expect, or even what you might offer in recompense.

People who join groups at the first opportunity often imagine that if they don't take the promises made at their induction seriously then no penalty can be exacted, so they then tend to ignore the details. If they boast about their occult activities and tell outsiders the names of group members and where and when the group meets, and reveal its god-names and other secret symbols, they will be in for an unpleasant surprise. Don't imagine for one moment that members of the group will turn up at midnight on your doorstep, intent on wreaking vengeance, because karma doesn't work like that. What will happen is that each time you need to trust someone, to rely on another's help, that trust will be betrayed. Friends might turn out to be two-faced, relationships lose their honesty. Trust and honour are two-edged swords: if you keep your word, then when it matters others will keep their promises to you. You may have come across the term 'warlock' as a sort of alternative for male witch, but what it really means is 'word-breaker', from the Anglo-Saxon *Waer-logga*. Ignorant male witches do sometimes call themselves warlocks, but as it means deceiver, and they are clearly deceiving themselves by never finding out the meaning of a term applied to themselves, the description is true. Would you care to saddle yourself with the title *gaeldorcraeftig*?

Betrayal of trust is the most common reason for people being cast out of groups, either quietly, by being told to leave, or not turn up for future meetings, or far more rarely, ceremonially banished from that company. A factor which lies at the heart of this dismissal is the matter of magical names. Pick up any American occult publication and you will find dozens of letters and articles from the Lady Moondust Unicorn, or Math ap Annwfyn, or Rainbowflower Goldendawn, and more exotic than that. These are clearly not the ordinary family names these people were given as children, so they must be adopted, magical names. One of the things that most oaths at the initiation into British magical groups demand that the candidate does not reveal are the magical names of members of the Order, including their own. In fact, the early Golden Dawn was so secretive that many of its members, who all had lengthy Latin or Greek mottoes as their magical names, were only known by the initials of those names, the whole motto being sealed in the vaults and known only to the Master of the Lodge and the individual. There is a good reason for this, for the name you take in magic, whether it is Marigold Moonstone, or *Nil Desperandum*, will cause a very powerful link to be forged between you and the inner worlds. Like Words of Power, such a name indicates your ambition and is for ever recorded on the Akashic Records. If only your brethren in lodge know it besides the gods or angels you serve, should you hear it being called you know that something very powerful is going on. If everyone in the street knows your secret name you will be ragged about it and it will be useless. Even if you work alone you may wish to take an inner name, to use when signing a talisman or making a request, but do be discreet, for the knowledge of secret names can give people a strong hold over each other. If someone tells you their magical motto, don't brag about it, honour their secret, and they will respect yours.

The situation is slightly different among witches for in some covens everyone is known by their 'magical' or 'craft' name.

Witch names are sometimes those of gods and goddesses, but to use such a title is rather arrogant, and it is also possible, that if you call yourself Bran the Blessed or Artemis someone else will invoke you! You can have this happen, and even if you don't realise it, you have to fulfil the task of the god whose name you have borrowed! It seems that nearly all the Gardnerian and Alexandrian covens go in for the most exalted names, people who belong to the rare 'Traditional' groups (who on the whole celebrate their festivals in quite a different way, and usually meet out of doors, robed, at sacred sites) choose names which are derived from nature. It is much safer, if you are a novice, to be called 'Oak' or 'Rosemary' than some high-falutin title to which you have no real claim.

Robes and regalia can provide further problems to beginners on the path. Most people are aware that some kinds of witches meet 'sky-clad', wearing only necklaces or headdresses, for example, because, having inherited much of their knowledge from warmer Mediterranean traditions, this was a reasonable thing to do. It does mean that most of their meetings are indoors. If power won't flow properly through a thin robe how is it supposed to pass through brick walls? Or should indoor witches only work for the benefit of those present in the circle? Lots of magical groups on other paths do wear at least a simple robe, and have no difficulty directing their energies from in or out of doors to benefit people at a distance, or the planet as a whole. Anyway, if you have never worn a long skirt before, and nearly all ceremonial attire is at least ankle-length, you will have to get used to the idea. Men may find it particularly strange to have to learn to walk about in a long frock, kneel, sit and stand without falling over, or tripping over the hem. It is another aspect of the practical side of magic which needs practice to make perfect. You may have to take care about long, loose sleeves, if there are lighted candles and incense about.

Not only is there the matter of wearing your robe, but of having it made, or making it yourself. Ideally you should sew it with your own fair hands, although the really desperate get their mothers to do it for them, or even resort to buying one from a supplier. Robes ought to be made of natural fibres like wool, cotton or silk, rather than anything man-made. Wool is warm and fairly fireproof, cotton is easy to wash, and silk feels gorgeous! Most shop robes are made of courtelle or some other modern cloth which is not so comfortable to wear, and is not as traditional as natural fibres. A simple kaftan needs only one seam sewn on each side, and should be loose and flowing. Colours vary: some older groups prefer all their members to wear black, others wear white, and many of the newer sorts of orders and robed covens go for all the colours of the rainbow. It does help to establish if your intended group has a particular colour if you are about to make or buy a robe. You will probably need a piece of coloured or white cord to go round your middle, and as in Judo, the different colours may indicate rank or office. Sometimes soft slippers are worn and some sort of headgear, but any decent lodge will explain how these are to be made, or help a novice to make them to their own pattern. You will need somewhere to hang your robes when not in use. Like magical names, lodge clothing is not to be worn to parties, or about in the street. That could be another reason for getting thrown out of a group!

You might find you have to carry things to meetings. Most witches have Athames. These are knives with black handles. They also have knives with white handles, which are used for cutting herbs and bread in the circle. The black ones are never used to cut anything physical, in the magical circle. Most lodges have at least one officer who carries a sword and these can produce transport problems too, as mentioned earlier. If the long arm of the law reaches out for you, you had better have a good story ready, especially as your oath of silence may well prevent you telling the truth of the matter. Perhaps you had better join a fencing club in order to have a handy disguise for your ritual apparel and equipment. If you do learn to fence, at least when you come to earn a magical sword, you will know how to use it, and not do any harm with it.

Maybe you have decided all this is too much, and that you do not wish to dance sky-clad before a High Priestess, representing the Moon Goddess, or burden yourself with the robes and regalia of ceremonial magic, what other options are there? Actually there are many. Apart from abandoning the occult ways altogether, which is one answer (although you do have to quell your natural curiosity as to what you might be missing), there are many peripheral arts and skills which are not so esoteric yet provide an opportunity at the very fringe of the unseen where you can live and work entirely in the mundane world.

The most obvious is the field of alternative therapies. There are dozens of these, from acupressure to zone therapy, through all the aspects of herbal medicine, naturopathy, homoeopathy, massage, applied kinesiology, iridology and the Bach Flower Remedies, to various sorts of purely spiritual healing, radionics, which works as an extension of dowsing, and many more therapies, both ancient and modern. Instructional courses are run in many of these healing arts, lasting from a few weekends to four years full-time at university. Although most of them have their own orthodoxy and methods, the kind of enhanced intuition that magical knowledge might have given you will always be an advantage. Radionics is almost entirely intuitive, whereas herbalism requires a profound knowledge of the many healing plants and their specific applications. If you think you might prefer the healing path to that of ordinary magical training, you will be able to discover schools offering appropriate instruction from any of the widely available magazines which deal with natural healing. You might discover there is a clinic in your nearest town where practitioners will be only too happy to explain their treatment methods and where training may be obtained.

In many cases, magical work will have its own aspect of healing. Most covens will certainly work for the recovery of any of their members and a properly trained ceremonial magician will know how to make a healing talisman or perform a ritual to restore wholeness. There are factors of responsibility even in something which seems to be as beneficially clear-cut as working for someone's good health, but certain matters do need to be borne in mind. There is the karmic factor. People do get ill for a variety of reasons. They may conduct their lives unhealthily, smoking, eating badly, taking drugs or overworking, and the sickness is a direct lesson to them to change themselves. A sudden recovery in which they do not assess their bad habits will not benefit them at all. In the case of old folk it is also necessary to exercise caution because, in all fairness, everyone's time will be up someday, and it may be better not to attempt using magic to prolong a life that is nearing its proper end. You must meditate and be certain, and if you can't decide that someone really needs your healing efforts, you can always ask the Gods to do what is best for the patient. It is necessary to be asked for help too, for simply practising on their illness is bad practice, and verging on interfering in their lives. An experienced magician or witch will know when someone is ready to die, and will be trained in the gentle arts of assisting that to happen, peacefully and quickly. The same applies, when it is your own turn. Even if you are young it is well worth meditating on death, reincarnation, or the afterlife. Make up your mind about heaven and hell, sin and forgiveness, and what the death process might be like. Get your magical affairs in order too.

A related subject to which you should give some thought is transplant surgery. Would you be happy to receive parts of some other individual to keep you alive if your heart, lungs, liver or kidneys were diseased? Would you wish to donate your eyes, heart, kidneys and liver should a sudden death overtake you? (If you die from anything except an accident or brain damage this won't apply, and you might be able to protect yourself from such fatal mishaps if you master magic!) If you believe that bits of you could help others after your death, then do go to the bother of carrying a donor card all the time, and tell your family that this is your wish. On the other hand, you might feel that if a part of you remained alive you might not be able to go on to your next incarnation, or get through the limbo stage to another level of the afterlife. Think about it.

Think too about the Spiritualists' teachings, of asking mediums to make contact with the dear departed and ask them how they are doing on the 'other side'. Would you like to get to your rest after a long and useful life, and find you are called upon to answer questions as to the state of your well-being, and what you did with the family silver? There is, certainly, a role in the magical healing field of comforting the bereaved, and the dying, but whether this should be taken a slightly ghoulish step further is something you need to investigate and then make up your own mind about. Spiritualism has some similarities with certain inner branches of magic, but the closed and psychically protected circle of the occult lodge is a rather different place to an unprotected public meeting hall. Mediumship of any sort is not something you should launch yourself into without careful consideration and proper training in the hands of people you really respect and trust. There are places your soul can stray to, beyond your ken, and there are lurking entities who would love the opportunity to get a foothold in this level of reality, so take care. It doesn't happen often, but if you ever enter a trance state – that is, when you have no control of your state of mind, and can remember nothing about it afterwards – get expert help. You always have some awareness in magical mind-states.

There are quite a few counselling tasks which can be performed by people who are properly trained thought not academically qualified. Hospices, where patients with terminal illnesses, young and old, go to die when their own families cannot cope with their nursing care, always need kind and thoughtful people to talk with these patients, smooth the way from life to death, or simply cheer them up. Now that AIDS is causing the death of many previously lively young people, there is a great need for others, who accept their unfortunate state, yet are willing to befriend them in their last days. If you feel this very unrewarded sort of service could be something you would be prepared to tackle you would be taking up one of the roles of the ancient priesthood. The same applies to things like dealing with drug abusers, taking round soup to the homeless at night, and all kinds of charity work. Most of it is unpaid, but like magical work, it is rewarded on inner levels. If you desire to travel but can't afford it, there are charities overseas who are always looking for volunteers to teach a language, help plant trees, dig wells, make roads and improve farming methods. If you cherish the Earth as your Mother then any sort of practical work, at home or abroad, which helps restore her fertility, to feed her children, your brothers and sisters, must be helping her. Offering love and service in these ways is just as important as sitting comfortably in your well-appointed lodge, asking angelic forces to aid you.

There are many similar tasks which you can find in Britain, especially if you respond to nature, and like ancient and sacred sites. Many of these places need to be cared for. This need not be done in a formal way, but if there is somewhere wild or sacred near your home, you could make it your duty to keep it looking and feeling its best. Remove rubbish, maintain any trees or fences, ensure that whoever owns it restores worn paths, or prevents buildings or other obstructions spoiling the views. Talk to people you encounter there, telling them about the place and its value to you. Learn about the local stones and plants. Join a conservation team, or a group studying local history. These organisations will often get you in to visit places which are not open to the general public. You can trace your family history through genealogy societies and may discover all sorts of fascinating things that way, helping you to acknowledge your value to society. Any exoteric club will provide you with friends and acquaintances who share at least part of your interest.

Another step in this direction is that of ecology. The Earth is our home, and magically, is seen as a living being. We are made from her substance, and as a great Mother Goddess, she is sacred. We should try to understand which human processes are harming

her, through chemical, nuclear or toxic wastes, through aerosol
chemicals which are destroying our protective ozone layer.
Human beings are killing trees, and causing other species to
become extinct *every day of the year*. We don't know the value of
every small insect, every tree, shrub, herb and vine for healing,
for natural contraception, for defeating cancer, but many plants
in tropical rain forests have such traditional uses. Some countries
are destroying stocks of mighty whales, of dolphins and other sea
mammals. These large, warm-blooded, intelligent creatures
deserve better than that. There are two ways of protecting them.
One is the magical way, by working on the inner levels, to change
the minds of politicians, in whose hands, ultimately, the fate of
these mighty sea creatures and forests rests. Perhaps they can be
encouraged to think again, through protests, by being inundated
with signed petitions, by mass marches, or because at last their
own Holy Guardian Angel, speaking to them with the voice of
conscience, tells them to make changes to laws. This sort of thing
can be effective, especially if the trained minds of witches and
magicians link together to request a re-examination of the data,
from the inner levels outwards. It won't work instantly – many
years may have to pass; but in the end there is a better chance that
things will be changed for the benefit of the entire planet.

This same inner pressure can be applied to the banishment of
nuclear weapons, and perhaps all nuclear materials. Unless the
Inner finds a way to store and decontaminate the ever-growing
stockpile of useless but deadly nuclear waste it can't be destroyed
until thousands of years pass to make it harmless! Wars can be
prevented if those who send the young men and women into the
battlefields discover the cost to themselves in karmic terms.
When wars cease then the battlefields may be turned again into
cornfields, and the technology of communication, transport,
irrigation, mass feeding, all so necessary to a war effort may be
correctly applied to a peace effort. Take an army and ask it to dig
trenches, not for protection, but for water to flow through, and
they will still dig. Require them to plant trees, not to fire rockets
or rifles, create camps for the sick and hungry, build dams and
water reservoirs, sow crops and in due time harvest them. The
army may not be able to make it rain, but if their prayers were for
a rain of water and not of bullets it would be certain to be
beneficial. Once trees and green things start to take root they can
change the climate for the better, in their turn shepherding rain-
bearing clouds over the dry lands. These miracles of rebirth have

happened in some places; the will exists, the knowledge exists, all that is lacking is the wisdom of those in high places who seem to prefer to see a field filled with the marching ranks of gravestones rather than fruit trees! Pray for them to gain wisdom.

You may not wish to travel so far from home, or work on seemingly difficult and distant projects, but you can improve your own garden, and plant wild flowers there, encourage birds and small animals to visit you for food and water. You can learn the history of your small plot and see what best use you can make of it. Perhaps you will cultivate herbs for healing and culinary purposes, for making incenses and pot-pourri, or grow fresh vegetables and fruit. These you can share as the Goddess's bounty, and if you love her she will reward you with healthy crops and tasty produce, which offers the greatest of communions between deities and you and your friends and family. You can ensure that you do not use harmful chemicals, weedkillers or pest-destroying products. You can experiment with organic methods, using companion planting so that bugs which affect one sort of plant are scared away by the smell of another, using Nature's own deterrents safely and naturally. Cultivate friendly birds and insects which can do a lot to prevent blights and the spoiling of crops, and grow plants to attract our ever-diminishing varieties of butterflies and moths. None of this is particularly 'occult' yet the knowledge is part of the inherited wisdom of the Cunning Man, the Wise Woman and the shaman, who knew the use and advantages of every plant and creature, for healing, for giving visions, or for nourishment of body and spirit. They would gain information from the familiar small animals, not by spoken words, but by behaviour, indicating important changes in the weather to come, or the arrival of food animals, or a crop of some wild fruit becoming ready. You can regain much of this forgotten wisdom if that is what you wish. Learn to be simple and appreciate things as they are, knowing their place in the universal scheme of things and not wanting change for change's sake.

Another non-ritual approach which might appeal to some people, especially those who have lived a full and interesting life, is taking up any of the other counselling arts, like the Chinese oracle of the I Ching, or astrology. Each is best studied by mature individuals who have the sense and sensitivity to understand how a client's problems can ruin his life. Certainly each has a wealth of literature to help understand the underlying system, but it is just as important to be able to feel for people, and know through personal experience what failure, change, trouble or illness can do to a previously well-ordered life. Astrology needs to be learned and fully understood. It isn't enough to buy an expensive computer program which will print out any birth-chart, interpret it, and give progressions as well. A computer cannot feel or interpret, and the interwoven planetary aspects, combined with the signs of the zodiac, and the house positions can produce totally individual situations in anyone's chart. The best astrologers use the process of establishing a natal chart as a way of tuning in to the person whose chart it is. As each planet is located, the natural relationships, easy or difficult, the hidden talents, the more obscure aspects of the individual's character slowly emerge.

Astrology takes years to master fully, for you first need to look thoroughly at your own life as it is indicated by your chart, appreciating exactly how each set of positions and aspects says things about your particular uniqueness. Only by seeing how each planet and house is reflected in the person you are, and what has occurred in your life can these things become clear in the charts of other people. It takes a lot of patience and consideration before the patterns speak clearly to you, and the essential information comes as second nature. Merely repeating what some computer programmer thinks might be relevant about a certain configuration detracts from the essential art of astrology, and does nothing for your reputation. All a client can say is that you have a reasonable computer, and that won't get *you* fame or fortune!

A working knowledge of astrology is an adjunct to much of the formal side of ceremonial magic. A talisman which needs to incorporate the influence of a particular planet will be more powerful if made when that planet is well-aspected. Rituals may take their energy from certain planets, particularly the Sun and the Moon (neither of which are actually planets outside the astrological term!) so that the work for physical healing may be done when the sun is in the sky, and rites for mental expansion or healing performed when a waxing moon is visible. Often the beneficial energies of several planets may be combined in a talisman for a special purpose, so it is necessary to wait until all the factors are in their best possible aspects to each other. For this reason a real Jupiter talisman, for example, could not be made when Jupiter was badly aspected – square to Saturn, for example. As some planets move very slowly you might be in for a long wait for something very special. If you know your basic astrology you will be able to appreciate these things. A mass-produced and therefore useless charm would not take any time to make, because its seller wouldn't be actually dedicating it to a particular planet. Do watch out!

The powers of the planets may be used in all sorts of ways, helping you to choose a colour, number, material, gem, incense, date, metal and all kinds of other things which should be attuned to bring forth the best results of any working. You may find, if you do go in for solo or small group rituals, that you need to build up a collection of different coloured robes or cords, candle holders in different metals, symbols, incenses and so on so that you are prepared to work with any planetary influence as the need arises. This is why magic takes so long to learn. It isn't a matter of looking things up in books, but of *knowing them*, in your head, so they can be applied at a moment's notice. This deep understanding comes only from continual study and practice, absorbing knowledge, until through the action of experience, it becomes true wisdom.

You can gain knowledge and understanding by asking reasonable questions and increasing your dealings with other people in that way. If you ask about the groups they belong to before they have mentioned the subject, you might get a very frosty answer. It is very much a matter of tact and learning just how far you can take your enquiries. Be prepared for both helpful and evasive answers. Many people are bound by traditional oaths of discretion, and many occultists are naturally cagey about their magical doings. You will also need to question yourself to be certain that each step you take along the twisting path is what you really want to do. Seizing every opportunity to join a new group, or attending every kind of instructional weekend, if you can afford it, might seem a good idea, but it is far better to choose one direction and stick to it, until you are certain it isn't right.

There are a number of national annual conferences run by magical groups, there are many festivals, New Age fairs and exhibitions where you can meet those from the esoteric world who acknowledge that they have a public function. You will be able to see and question people who sell magical equipment, blend incenses, make special charms and offer helpful publications. You can meet many other Seekers, and over a cup of tea and a bean sprout sandwich, you can ask them how they are getting on. It is often through these seemingly 'co-incidental' meetings that the basis for an enduring friendship may be formed.

Many of those people who attend public gatherings are just as lost as you may be, and will be delighted to encounter others who have the same feelings. Magic is always a lonely road, and as you will have seen, the simplest questions have the most complex answers. Finding a few companions, young or old, experienced or beginners, members of a training school, perhaps, or loners who have not found their preferred way, will offer you support. The way through the labyrinth is difficult – it always was; but thousands of people have trodden those entangled and hidden roads, through the worlds, both seen and unseen.

There are strong networks of communication in the magical world too. Once you meet people who know others, they can direct you, and put you in touch with groups near your home, or with postal training schools of good reputation and sound experience. They will also monitor your activities, so if you decide to go round and join lots of fellowships, groups and covens and imagine no one will know, you will be in for a surprise! Although many traditions and schools are totally separate, and many do not allow their members to join other groups at the same time, there is a strong bond of old friendships running through most of the British and many American orders and societies, covens and schools. News soon gets round that 'Peter Black' is joining one or two or more organisations, and you might get asked some very awkward questions! There are very close communications links between occult groups, on a variety of levels, from the most mundane, where members of different schools read each others' magazines, to the inner links of descended power where later orders have grown out of earlier ones, some going back, in various incarnations for hundreds of years. There is a lot of love, affection, trust, good humour and dedication among any collection of experienced occultists, no matter how different their chosen paths may be. You will find people hugging each other, and their smiles show it is not mere politeness.

All magical work is ultimately that of service. Service to mankind, service to Mother Nature, service to Creation and service to your evolving self. That duty is not rewarded with fame or fortune, nor with material gains, except as a kind of side-effect, but such dedication, honestly made, will ultimately bring you joy, respect, responsibility, humility, friendship, and perhaps honour. You cannot buy these gifts, only earn them. If you accept the difficult path, which I have tried to explain, you

will gain wisdom and many blessings from the gods and goddesses you serve, who will bring you health, and happiness, and
eventually, the accomplishment of your True Will. If you prefer
to turn your back on the magical path, and make your own way
in the world, you will be able to strive for mundane success,
material wealth, power, but you will not have the experiences,
nor, perhaps, gain the same kind of wisdom. We all have absolute
choice. One road leads inwards, to the maze at the heart of our
inner castle; the other road, scattered with jewels and the remains
of burned-out failures, leads to the world of everyday toil and
achievement. You are standing at that crossroads, and guided by
whatever steps you may already have taken on both of those
ways, now you may go forward on your chosen path. In either
direction you will know that you are not alone.

End Word

If you are one of those people who turns to the end of the book first, this is what you have missed by not reading all of it – this book deals with the many choices which a novice who wants to be a magician or witch will have to face. Some of the details, written as the result of many years working in several branches of the Western Mystery Tradition, have never been revealed before. These are the kind of thing no one tells you, but that you have to discover for yourself. This does not mean that by merely reading this book you will have all the power and wisdom you demand, but that you will have the basic *understanding* to fathom out what people mean, what exercises are supposed to assist you to do, and what is supposed to happen when, for example, you meditate. Of course, if you have already been studying for some time you may know what is spelled out here, and your own experience may be similar, or perhaps quite different – magical life is like that.

Be very certain that no matter what films and books may suggest, the only rewards for magical work, of any sort, on any path, have to be earned by the sweat of your own brow. Power and wisdom cannot be purchased, nor sacrificed for, nor extracted by threat, nor given to you by someone else, no matter what they might promise in advertisements! What you gain will be all your own work. It can take years, it can take lives, in some cases it may never be achieved, just as you wish. You will have to learn who you are, where you have come from and what your true needs are, and that is only the first step towards discovering your True Will.

You will have to accept, to begin with, that there are other levels of awareness which you can train yourself to reach, wherein you encounter the Gods, your Holy Guardian Angel, the Akashic Records, the heroes and wizards of myth and legend, truly living in their own realms. You will develop skills, to far-see, to divine, to heal and to control your inner keys to power. You will learn vast amounts of ancient lore, strange alphabets, the art of story-telling, and even of entering fully that 'Other-world' to interact with what you find there. You will develop your awareness of the Creator, your religious ideas about wor-ship and communion, festivals and thanksgiving ceremonies. Once you safely hold the key, which is the only control you may ever have, which opens the inner doors of the mind, you can explore all time and space, reality as you know it, and the lands of legend. That is the true secret of any kind of successful magic. I can tell you that, but you cannot just do it! You will need to find a way which works for you, and there are many of those to choose from. Learning such a skill takes time, so does any ordinary skill. How long does it take to learn to play a musical instrument well? How long to become fluent in another language? That is very similar to the magical path, for you need to understand and correctly apply all the technical words, the jargon of occultism, both within your own training, and when dealing with other people. If you attend lectures on the 'Cosmic Doctrine' and hear about Lords of Flame, Lords of Form and the Ring Pass Not, what will you make of it? What about the true meaning of 'warlock', or how would you consult the I Ching, and where would you get a ticket for the Akashic Record library?

Words cannot explain these things to you. Magical power comes entirely from a combination of practical knowledge – which you gain as you go along, intuition – which is developed once you get a hold on your inner mind, wisdom – which is the combination of these two, and finally experience. 'The Proof of the Talisman is in its effectiveness!' Until you have tried all the exercises a few dozen times, and failed to get results a few dozen times, and then mysteriously succeeded just when you were about to give up, you cannot *know* anything about magic. Only when you start to succeed more often than you fail will you begin to build up confidence in the exercise and benefit from the results it produces. Then magic enters a new dimension. It requires *very hard work*, and will only produce instant results after about five years of regular practice! If you are not willing to offer dedication, effort, time and energy, to study, to sit quietly and think, to dress up in strange robes and ask for help from invisible beings, or to encounter the Old Gods within a coven or in the wild places, then this is not the path for you. Turn back now to the comfort and security of the mundane world, and strive to be successful there. You won't need to work so hard or long. The Path through the Labyrinth is available to all who choose to follow it, but what you may discover in the centre may not be what you most wish for before you set out. The maze will change you, for it causes the powers of inner evolution to work increasingly on you and your life. Magic will change you, and you might not like the result. The clues to the safest path are here, but you alone may open the gate to your own experience. It is right in front of you, now. Good luck.

Marian Green, Bath, January 1988

Glossary

There are a number of specialist words used throughout this book which may be unfamiliar to you. Some of them may well have dictionary definitions but the explanations given here are intended to express what I mean by each term, and this may differ.

adept	An experienced and competent practitioner of the magical arts.
Akashic Records	A library of information about every living thing on Earth which may be consulted mentally about your past lives and forgotten wisdom.
altar	A table on which magical instruments, tools and symbols are laid out during a magical ceremony.
alternative therapies	Any of the variety of healing methods applied by trained practitioners which are not part of orthodox medicine, for example acupuncture, reflexology or spiritual healing.
angels	Vast immortal beings from whom help or guidance may be requested.
anima/animus	Terms used by Carl Jung to describe aspects of

	our souls which are of the opposite sex.
Annwn	A Celtic name for the Otherworld, where reality is created.
Aquarian Age	The next Great Sign of the Zodiac into which our solar system will fully enter in about 200 years. We are at present in the end of Pisces, but are already experiencing some of the changes associated with the coming New Age.
arcane	Usually applied to magical knowledge, meaning ancient and hidden.
Archangels	Raphael, Gabriel, Michael and Auriel/Uriel, often requested to guard the four quarters in High Magic.
archetype	Again an expression used by Jung to define a particular kind of legendary character, like the Old Wise Woman, often encountered in dreams or visions.
Arts	The Arts are the practical skills gained through study and practice, like the art of divination, each requiring mental and physical expertise.
ASCs	Altered States of Consciousness, in which the awareness is directed to the theme of a meditation or pathworking which can be entered and terminated totally under control of the meditator.
astral	A real world on a different plane of existence to our everyday experience. Can be entered whilst in an ASC – astral travel.
Athame	A black-handled ceremonial knife, used by many modern witches.
Atlantis	A lost civilisation, thought to have sunk under the Atlantic Ocean many thousands of years ago, but where many magical arts and philosophies of the West have their spiritual roots.
aura	An energy field surrounding all living things, made up of fine rainbow-coloured filaments, visible to trained people.
banishing ritual	A magical ceremony performed to psychically purify the area within a circle, around an individual or a house. Will disperse

everything, so needs to be revoked at the end!

Bards   The ancient order of Celtic story-tellers and historians who brought information and music to the common people.

biofeedback   A system of scientific measurement in which a sound or dial will indicate to the meditator the depth of his relaxation.

black magic   Selfish and ultimately self-destructive arts which compel individuals or situations, always against the evolution of the spirit.

blessing   The practice of making a thing holy or set apart, usually with a ritual gesture (Sign of the Cross, etc.) or a full ceremony.

brain   The physical organ controlling the body, divided almost in half, with logical and linear thinking on the left side, spacial, intuitive consciousness on the right side. Magical work balances both hemispheres.

breathing   Breathing in slow, regular patterns is often used to aid relaxation before meditation. It can induce ASCs.

candidate   Literally 'One in White', applicant for initiation.

candles   Real flames in lamps or candles are used to change the atmosphere for many kinds of magical working, divination or ritual.

cauldron   A large iron cooking-pot, often placed at the centre of modern witches' circles, forerunner of the Holy Grail.

ceremonial magic A complex system of symbolism, often based on the Qabalah, used by High Magicians as opposed to low magicians or witches.

ceremony   An elaborate ritual, formally set out, often with several participants, for a specific purpose, e.g. initiation.

channelling   A form of mediumship which is becoming very popular. Dangerous if untrained people allow beings from other levels of creation to take over their entire consciousness, in order to pass on messages or spiritual guidance. When controlled, can be experienced as a form of inspiration.

chanting	A system of making rhythmic verbal sounds in order to change your state of consciousness or empower a spell.
charms	These are natural magical objects like fossils or stones which have mysterious powers. Amulets ward off harm and are eye-shaped charms. A spoken charm is used to heal or communicate with nature – charming the birds out of the trees. Low magic.
circle	A consecrated (blessed) place used by witches and magicians to outline their working space and contain its power.
Communion	A shared meal of bread, biscuit, salt and wine, water or mead. Its origins are of great antiquity, used to seal the bonds of companionship at the end of a ceremony.
consciousness	A normal state of awareness which can be altered at will in order to enter ASCs and so perceive other levels of reality.
correspondences	Lists of colours, objects, incenses and so on, specifically linked with a particular planet or sign of the zodiac. Used to empower a talisman, or focus a ritual on a specific purpose.
cosmos	The entire visible universe, from galaxies down to the tiniest atom of material earth, seen as a coherent whole.
coven	A gathering of thirteen or less modern witches. (There is little historic evidence that actual covens existed in Britain before this century.) Usually directed by a High Priestess.
creative visualisation	Using trained aspects of consciousness to create images, scenes and changes in what you desire to happen. Properly applied 'imagination' (making images) is the greatest power in modern magic.
crystal ball	A crystal or glass sphere used to distract the attention so that you can enter the correct ASC in order to be able to see at a distance, or into the future. A speculum.
Cunning Man	An old title for a male solo witch, or perhaps shaman, found in eastern Britain in the last

century. A Horse Doctor.

cup

Symbol of the element water, used in the communion, also a recollection of the Holy Grail in the Western Mystery Tradition.

dabbler

A person who does not have the self-discipline to study a system of magic, or anything else, thoroughly. A danger to himself and those associated with him, due to releasing uncontrolled energies within his life. Someone who flits from group to group, not really learning anything useful.

Dark

The lack of Light, a mental state of ignorance, a force which true magic will strive to balance. You can't have day without night, summer without winter.

dedication

This is a formal, if secret, commitment to following an occult path, and can take the form of self-initiation into the Mysteries. It is also the determination to carry the aim through.

deity

God or goddess.

divination

The arts of 'Gaining information from Divine Sources', usually using the Tarot, the I Ching, the Runes or any similar skill. A diviner is one who may be seeking information, like the position of water, or knowledge from the Gods, to help others who come for advice or answers to questions.

dowser

An old word for a 'water diviner', usually implying the use of a dowsing twig or pendulum.

dreams

Important messages received from your inner or subconscious mind, well worth recording and examining, may be predictions.

drugs

Drugs which alter consciousness are never used in modern magical work. You need total personal control. Most systems of alternative medicine use natural herbs rather than drugs.

Druid

An ancient priesthood of the Celtic People in Europe, before about 600 AD, whose sacred places were oak groves.

dryad

A term used by folk magicians to describe the

	group souls of trees, who may help those who request aid.
dual consciousness	A state of awareness, common in meditation, etc., when you are partly aware of where you are actually sitting, and partly focused on the theme of the meditation or pathworking scene.
ecology	This is the study of the interaction of mankind with the planet Earth. Ecologists strive to conserve natural environments, wild animals, plants and forests. If you worship Mother Nature, it is wise to understand the need for care and conservation. Mankind could become an extinct species too, through his own greed and folly.
Elements	Earth, water, fire and air are magically considered to be the four constituents of matter – particles, fields, energy and forces are what the physicists see them as. Often used to mark out and bless a magical circle. The Elementals are natural beings associated with each of these elements, who are from another order of creation. They can be encountered if you are willing to seek them out in their own environment, but they will not necessarily co-operate with you.
Enlightenment	The result of the quest for wisdom, which can sometimes produce spectacular flashes of understanding after many weeks of hard labour
Enochian	An ancient language, often used in High Magic but not safe for novices to experiment with.
entity	A being from another dimension, often unpleasant, and given to infesting those who make themselves open, through untrained mediumship, black magic and the like. Needs expert removal!
equipment	Ritual tools, furniture, symbolic weapons, items for the Communion, all kept aside for purely magical use. Usually specially blessed before use.

esoteric	Another term like occult, which infers a specialist knowledge, or out of the ordinary subject. Matters of spiritual value rather than those of the world.
evocation	A request which calls up deeper levels within a person or the cosmos. You can try evoking Elementals. Opposite to invocation.
exorcist	A highly trained priest or occultist, skilled in the arts of communicating with, controlling and expelling entities, usually by ritual means. Not a task for a novice.
exoteric	Outer, worldly matters, as opposed to esoteric or secret ones.
Faery	The hidden kingdom of the Otherworld. Now sometimes used to describe American covens of gay, male witches.
far memory	Another term used to describe past-life recall or reincarnation research. Used when you consult the Akashic Records.
fellowship	A name given to a society with formal conditions of membership, originally all men, but now mixed, for example the Goddess-orientated Fellowship of Isis.
folklore	The unwritten and ancient tradition, handed down to us in songs, poetry and folk customs, yet which retains the keys to our native tradition.
Freemasonry	A society with secrets based on the mystical aspects of the building of King Solomon's Temple in Jerusalem. Originally for men, working on sacred buildings, but now there are mixed Lodges of Co-Masons, and an Order of Women Freemasons, who study and practise speculative, ceremonial masonry.
ghosts	The shadows of dead people, somehow locked into the scene of their life or death, by a kind of tape recording into the fabric of the building, etc. Visible to animals and psychics.
Glastonbury	A small town in Somerset, near Bristol, in the West Country, famous for its strange hill, the Tor, which has pagan and Christian associations. A place of pilgrimage and it has

	been referred to as the 'Holyest Earth in England', because it may be one of the places where the Holy Grail was hidden. Also associated with King Arthur, and the site of the first Christian Church in England.
gods/goddesses	A variety of beings whose presence can be detected, and whose aid can be requested, within their own plane of existence. Aspects of the Creative Spirit.
Golden Dawn	The Hermetic Order of the Golden Dawn was founded at the end of the nineteenth century by a number of advanced Freemasons, based on some German cypher documents. Most of the Orders of High Magic can trace their roots back to this original Order, or one of its members' offshoot societies. The Golden Dawn still exists in America, run by the Israel Regardie Foundation.
Grail	The Holy Grail is a Christian version of a pagan Sacred Cup or Cauldron. It is also the inner goal of a personal magical quest, the path to initiation in the Western Mystery Tradition.
grimoire	A medieval magical textbook – the Key of Solomon for example.
group	A collection of working magicians, either formal like a lodge or coven of witches, or a loose-knit gathering of friends, studying and working together.
Guardians	Inner aspects of ourselves who prevent us doing things on the inner levels which might harm us. May appear during pathworkings, holding shut doors, or defending us from entities.
Guides	Again, aspects of our inner selves, linked to the Akashic Records, who will lead us through their realms of the Inner Worlds, give information, guidance or advice, or even inspiration.
guru	An Indian word for a holy teacher, usually sought in a remote place, who offers advice like 'All knowledge is within, go home!'

Hallowe'en

Festival at the end of October celebrating the end of summer and the start of the Celtic New Year. Important to witches as it is a time when the veil between past and future is thin. Also folk festival of ghosts and disguises, Trick or Treat in America.

healer

One who by drawing on his own links with Creation can heal others, either by herbs, alternative medicine or spiritual healing. Works on himself, people and animals.

heathen

Originally one who lived 'on the heath', a non-Christian.

herbs

Wild or cultivated plants or trees, used for medicine, in baths, to flavour food, as incenses and for making perfumes, and in divination.

Hermetic Tradition

The complex system of High Magic, based on the theories of Hermes Trismegistos, developed in the Middle Ages, involving ritual, symbolism, arcane philosophy and much more.

High Magic

As opposed to low magic which is folk magic and very simple, High Magic is an involved system of ritual, mental training, knowledge of correspondences, and is very formal.

High Priest/ Priestess

The leading male and female members of a modern coven, responsible for blessing a circle, performing initiations and directing the rituals at Sabbats (major festivals) and Esbats (Full Moon meetings). The High Priestess is usually the primary celebrant.

Holy Guardian Angel

An inner link we all have with the Creator, with whom we can train ourselves to communicate. Often speaks with the voice of our conscience, but can teach esoteric wisdom.

Horse Doctor

One of the names by which old-fashioned witches were known, famous for healing animals, especially horses by being able to communicate with them. Also called Horse Whisperers.

hypnogogic state   A natural state between waking and sleeping,

	a very useful ASC once you have learned to control it, and prolong it through meditation and pathworking.
I Ching	A Chinese oracle; a system of divination which is very old.
image	A scene or object held within the mind's eye.
imagination	The most powerful tool a modern magician has, for in this aspect of inner creativity we are able to work magic, heal, visit other places, other times on Earth, and other levels.
incense	Scented gums, woods, herbs and resins, burned on charcoal, or as joss-sticks, to enhance changes in atmospheres.
incubation	The ancient tradition of healing sleep, often hypnotically induced, wherein a patient dreamed of his cure.
initiate	One who has gone through the formal ceremony of initiation, either within a group or tradition, or through self-initiation.
Inner Planes	Inner realms of reality, entered whilst in controlled ASCs, where it is possible to gain information from the Inner Plane Adepts, who may be the evolved souls of dead magicians.
inner self	Another term for the anima or animus. The part of us most capable of evolving, healing us and making us wise.
inspiration	A direct form of knowledge, literally 'breathed in' which can be expressed in poetry, art, writing or other form of creativity, a direct gift from the Goddess.
instruments	The traditional weapons of High Magic, the sword, cup, wand and pentacle or shield.
intuition	An inner sense of knowledge, gained without learning, a feeling of unprompted certainty, and a valuable asset to all occultists.
invocation	The art of calling down help from higher sources, angels and evolved beings. The opposite of evocation.
Journeys	Inner Journeys are the simplest forms of pathworking, when it is possible to perceive, with your mind's eye, another scene, into

which you enter in search of knowledge, guidance, etc.

karma   The immutable law by which the good and harmful things you do in life are rewarded or paid for. It cannot be avoided.

Key of Solomon   Medieval textbook, still available, setting out the magical instruments, talismans, rituals and symbols still used in High Magic.

King Arthur   Legendary hero and sacred king, brought up by the magician Merlin. A key figure in the Grail legend and Sacred Quest, often encountered in dreams and visions. Defender of Britain.

knowledge   The first part of the process of becoming wise requires the acquisition of knowledge, by actually reading, learning and experiencing things. Magicians *know*, others *believe!*

labyrinth   A symbol for the twisting and confusing path towards wisdom and entry into magical initiation, originally the home of the Minotaur, slain by Theseus with help from Ariadne.

lamen   A ceremonial badge or sacred symbol, usually worn on a cord or chain round your neck, may indicate office or rank.

lamp   There is always a real flame in a lamp or candle lantern whilst any Lodge meeting or coven circle is in progress. Stands in for the Divine Light.

Left-Hand Path   Magical path to self-destruction, no matter what the adverts or novels might say. Anti-evolutionary magic.

legends   A vast array of tales and myths, which may not agree entirely with history, because many of the stories have a symbolic rather than a material basis. Have preserved much of our pre-literate initiation ceremonies.

Light   A symbolic term indicating an indefinable sort of wisdom, power, holiness or love, which strives to balance the Dark.

lodge   A group of ceremonial or high magicians, or the place in which they hold their rituals. Can

	be a temple.
mage/magus	Term for a competent magician, or Master of a lodge.
magic	The art of understanding and controlling change, in consciousness, and in the world at large.
magick	A pretentious term, coined by Aleister Crowley, to separate magic from stage conjuring, but now used by many who follow Crowley, or in America, High Magic in general.
Masters	Other-plane beings who offer instruction, or guidance, sometimes through channelling or inspiration.
mediation	The art of receiving information from Inner Plane sources, either the Inner Plane Adepts or deep aspects of yourself.
meditation	A state of controlled ASC wherein you are able to explore and expand information around a particular theme. A passive state, allowing information to seep in.
Merlin	A legendary wizard, Britain's magical guardian, whose life, legends and magic are still keys to the Western Mysteries.
mind-training	Most forms of magical practice, from meditation to rituals require a trained and focused mind. Many of the basic skills are methods of bringing more of the inner levels of the mind into awareness and under conscious control.
names	All words have power; names of individuals, especially the magical names taken or conferred at initiation give power over the person whose name it is. These should be secret and chosen with care and forethought.
native tradition	This is any land's original magical tradition, grown from the rocks and soil and explored by the original people. It is usually available in songs, tales, creation stories and the deeds of the local gods/heroes. Very basic and direct magic.
nature	The whole, untamed forces of the Earth. The

Earth Mother or Mother Nature is a great goddess who rules over these.

neophyte — Literally 'newly born', from the Greek, a recently initiated Seeker, or follower of High Magic.

New Age — The Age of Aquarius, also in a wider sense, changes in our awareness of subjects like ecology, alternative medicine, education, religion, self-discovery and direction.

novice — A Student or Seeker who has yet to be initiated, and who has only recently begun to study seriously and do some of the practical work, often on his own.

oath — A serious promise to obey certain rules, usually about silence or discretion concerning who, where and when any group meets, and a vow to work in harmony with it. May have seemingly serious penalties, and should *always be taken seriously!*

occult — Means 'hidden', and covers all sorts of knowledge, practices, arts and groups. Anything secret.

Old Religion — A name used by Traditional Witches for their faith. Pre-Christian pagan rites and gods and goddesses, and their worship.

oracle — A specially trained person, or divination system, which will accurately foretell future events.

Order — A well-established High Magic society.

Otherworld — The inner level of reality, where magical work has to be rooted, sometimes called 'Annwn' or the Underworld or Faery.

Outer Court — A public and approachable part of an Order, wherein students receive their initial training before admittance or initiation.

out of the body experience — A 'scientific' term for astral travel, an advanced ASC, where consciousness is totally projected out of the body, to some other place/time. Can happen in dreams.

pagan — Originally Latin for 'country-dweller', but now applied to people who have chosen to follow the Old Religion, or worship any gods and goddesses outside the orthodox religions.

pantacle   A magical talisman incorporating a pentacle (see below).

pantheon   A family of gods and goddesses in a particular time or place.

past-life recall Discovering who you were in previous incarnations, by consulting the Akashic Records, or through ASCs or pathworking.

pathworking   Originally a Qabalistic practice, exploring the paths of the Tree of Life, but now used as a general term for 'Inner Journeys', or Guided Meditations, following a symbolic or real road through inner worlds, to discover new information about yourself, or receive direction from a Guide, etc. Creative visualisation is another term used by psychologists, often using it for healing, seeing diseases being overcome, etc.

pentacle   A symbol of Earth, or a magical talisman sometimes used as a platter, with a five-pointed star on it.

Piscean Age   The period we are in now, according to the precession of the Great Signs of the Zodiac. Will end in about 200 years.

power   A general term for the energy called to our control by the arts of magic or ritual. Some comes through us from our inner links with the forces of Creation. Magic is the control of this, and its direction to heal, guide and inspire us.

projection of   A state of consciousness wherein it is possible
consciousness   to explore other real places, or other times, without losing total awareness of our bodies, and being able to talk, too.

psyche   Our inner sense and soul, which is naturally psychic.

psychic attack   The feeling of being overlooked or affected badly by some external force, which, in practice, is nearly always caused by something we have done. Uncontrolled psychic experiments, or too much banishing can lead to this experience. In rare cases of actual attack, expert help is required.

Qabalah   Often spelled Kabbala, Cabala, Cabbala, etc.
                   Originally a Hebrew oral tradition of teach-
                   ing, based on the Tree of Life.

quarters   It is usual to mark the four points of the
                   compass, north, south, east and west, in most
                   magical circles, in High Magic and witchcraft.

Quest   A real or symbolic journey in pursuit of
                   wisdom, the search for self-identity and
                   external power, in the Western Mystery
                   Tradition.

reader   One who gives advice from the Tarot, etc. A
                   diviner.

realisation   The sudden explosion of knowledge brought
                   about through meditation. A mental link is
                   formed and you say 'Aha!'

regalia   Magical robe, sandals, headdress, cord and
                   lamen, etc.

reincarnation   The theory of living many lives, evidence and
                   experience of which may sometimes be
                   discovered through magical arts.

relaxation   A vital aspect of all magical work – physical
                   calm and relaxation combined with mental
                   alertness leads into the requisite ASCs.

religion   A personal awareness of your relationship
                   with the Gods, the Creator, through either
                   orthodox faith, or personal discovery.
                   Worship, celebration and thanksgiving.

remote viewing   A scientific term for 'far-seeing', protection of
                   awareness.

responsibility   The greatest ethical force in magic. You are
                   totally responsible, not only for your
                   immediate magical activities, but for the
                   short- and long-term outcome of them. Learn
                   to be very careful and harm no one in your
                   occult work.

Right-Hand Path   The path of magical evolution, working in
                   harmony with the Laws of Creation.

rites of passage   Originally ceremonies in many lands to
                   celebrate births, deaths, marriages and
                   namings, now a term used to imply
                   initiations, or rituals to confer status or
                   degrees within the esoteric rather than

	exoteric world.
ritual	Another word for ceremony or rite. A formal working with one or more participants, for a predetermined objective.
robe	An ankle-length kaftan-shaped garment, worn by men and women in many groups and some covens, preferably home-made from silk, cotton or wool.
Runes	An ancient Anglo-Saxon and Germanic alphabet, with about twenty-four signs, used as a form of divination or as a magical script.
school	This is a well-established group which offers training, by post or in person, to many students who wish to follow its particular tradition, some of whom may later join the Outer Court and eventually be initiated.
scrying	An old name for crystal-gazing.
Seeker	Anyone who seriously pursues magical knowledge, or who seeks the Light of Wisdom.
self	The inner evolving aspect of your individual character.
self-initiation	If you cannot find a group to admit you, or you prefer to work alone, you can devise and perform a Ritual of Dedication, or Self-Initiation. Many magicians and witches now do this.
Shadow	The hidden or forgotten side of your inner nature, wherein the remains of failures, difficulties and bad habits may lie, which self-awareness encourages you to examine and deal with. The lower, more instinctive aspects of your character.
shaman	A popular term for a sorcerer, an individual folk magician, based on the idea of Red Indian or Siberian magic-workers, healers and practitioners of traditional arts of inherited knowledge and psychic power.
shrine	A personal sacred place or altar where you make requests or offerings, usually within a house or garden.
sigil	A magical letter or symbol.

skill	An acquired, practical ability, or inherent talent.
society	An established magical group with a formal constitution.
soul	The part of us which reincarnates and evolves. A *group soul* is built up within any regularly meeting group of people, and may link in with the group soul of a nation or land. The collective unconscious.
spell	A spoken or created magical charm, should be made for the time and purpose by those involved.
spirit	The evolving inner aspect of everyone. Spiritual matters are those which help it to go forward.
symbols	Designs, pictures, letters, shapes and images which have an ancient and wide-ranging meaning, far beyond themselves.
talisman	An elaborately made charm, based on the correspondences of a particular aim or planetary power. Make your own for best results!
Tarot	A set of image cards, originally seventy-eight, used for divination.
temple	A sacred place, either created within a building, or perceived within an inner world. The location of most rituals.
Threefold Return	A karmic law which states that if you do harm to anyone, consciously or unconsciously, you will have to pay by your own suffering three times over. Good is also returned three times. You cannot avoid this law of magic.
time-travel	A form of pathworking where you go back to the past, or even forward, usually looking at other Lives.
Tradition	A particular system of magical thought, usually linked to a specific place or time, i.e. Egyptian or Hermetic.
Tree of Life	An important symbol in Qabalistic studies, with ten Spheres of creation, joined by thirty-two paths, representing planetary energies and associated god-forms.

unconscious	The deeper part of our mind, usually beyond our waking awareness, but which can be explored through dream symbolism and meditation.
universe	The physical, visible interlinked system of stars, galaxies and planets.
'vibes'	A subtle sensation or atmosphere surrounding people or things, often strange or unsettling.
vigil	A period of separation, contemplation and withdrawal, usually before an initiation or important ceremony.
village witch	The original sort of folk-healer, green magician, Wise Woman, herbalist and pagan. The British 'shaman', and solo practitioner.
virtue	The magical ability of a herb or charm to work.
visions	The scenes and images conjured up before the inner eye, or free-flowing pictures which it perceives.
wand	A magician's staff of office, through which he may direct the power of his will.
warlock	'A lie-teller' literally, from the Saxon, but sometimes used by ignorant male witches.
Wasteland	The world we live in, desperately in need of restoration, by magical ingenuity and ecologically sound care. The Holy Grail will restore its green-ness, if it can be found.
weapons	Sword, cup, pentacle and wand.
Western Mystery Tradition	The store of inner knowledge, secrets and mysterious power of Britain and Western Europe, expressed in ancient legends, folk traditions and inherent wisdom. The Mysteries can be laid before ordinary folk as Mystery Plays but they will see only entertainment; the wise will understand the sacred or magical message.
white magic	Any form of healing, beneficial or responsible magic.
Wicca	An American term for witchcraft or its adherents, based on an Anglo-Saxon word.
will	True magical knowledge or objectives.
wisdom	Knowledge and experience combined to be

greater than both.

Wise Woman   Village witch, midwife or healer/herbalist.

witchcraft   The many talents of witches, some of whom today are members of covens. Pagans who celebrate festivals, full moons, and may work magic, perform divinations and healing. Practical skills of Low rather than ceremonial magic.

Words of Power   May be invocations, or spells, or names, including people's magical names which give control over certain things, like the names of certain gods/goddesses/angels, or sometimes words spoken in an ancient language, like Enochian. If you come across these and don't know exactly what is meant, *do not use them*. Watch out, too, in case your magical names are called out by someone else.

workshops   One- and two-day seminars involving talks by experts as well as actual, practical work, under the supervision of those who know how such exercises are supposed to be performed. One of the fastest and best ways of getting practical experience and information, firsthand, in an intensive way. Two days of proper instruction can save six months solo fumbling efforts, and you have the consolation of not being the only novice!

zodiac   The twelve signs or constellations which make up a circle in the heavens. It is the position of the ten planets, including the Sun and Moon, at your place and moment of birth which makes your horoscope unique. Knowledge of the signs of the zodiac, and the planets, forms the basis of much talismanic magic, and planetary positions may need to be checked when consecrating a talisman or performing a ritual. There is also the Glastonbury Zodiac, a great circle of figures, about thirty miles across, in Somerset, where the positions of the actual zodical constellations are set out in the countryside as great figures, marked in very ancient times by streams, tracks, hedges, earthworks, mounds, springs and clumps of trees. Even the village names are relevant: for example Babcary – meaning 'Child of Ceres (Demeter, corn goddess)' is the village in which the sign of Virgo lies. Other Earth Zodiacs are being investigated as well.

Bibliography

Many of the authors whose works are listed below have written a number of similar books, but these are the most helpful to novices. New books are always being published, so write to the publishers for a catalogue if there is no good bookshop near you.

Margot Adler, *Drawing Down the Moon*, USA.
Dolores Ashcroft-Nowicki, *First Steps in Ritual*, Aquarian.
    Highways of the Mind, Aquarian.
    Ritual Magic Workbook, Aquarian.
    The Shining Paths, Aquarian, 1983.
J. H. Brennan, *Astral Doorways*, Aquarian.
    Reincarnation: Five Keys to Past Lives, Aquarian.
W. E. Butler, *Apprenticed to Magic*, Aquarian.
J. and S. Farrar, *Eight Sabbats for Witches*, Hale.
    The Life and Times of a Modern Witch, Hale.
Sir James Frazer, *The Golden Bough*.
Dion Fortune, *The Sea Priestess* (Novel), Aquarian.
    The Training and Work of an Initiate, Aquarian.
G. B. Gardner, *The Meaning of Witchcraft*.
    Witchcraft Today.
W. G. Gray, *Ladder of Lights*, Aquarian.
Tom Graves, *The Diviner's Handbook*, Aquarian.
    Towards a Magical Technology, Aquarian.
Marian Green, *The Gentle Arts of Aquarian Magic*, Aquarian.
    Magic for the Aquarian Age, Aquarian.

Marian Green and J. Matthews, *The Grail Seeker's Companion*, Aquarian.

Christine Hartley, *The Western Mystery Tradition*, Aquarian.

Helene Hess, *The Zodiac Explorer's Guide*, Aquarian.

Murry Hope, *Practical Egyptian Magic*, Aquarian.
   Practical Techniques of Psychic Self-Defence, Aquarian, 1983.
   The Psychology of Ritual, Element.

Naomi Humphrey, *Meditation – the Inner Way*, Aquarian.

Brian Inglis, *Natural Medicine*, Granada.

Carl Jung, *Memories, Dreams, Reflections*, Fontana.

Gareth Knight, *The Secret Tradition in Arthurian Legend*, Aquarian.

T. C. Lethbridge, *Ghost and Divining Rod*.
   Gogmagog.

Caitlin Matthews, *Mabon and the Mysteries of Britain*, Arkana, RKP.

John Matthews, *The Grail – Quest for the Eternal*, Thames & Hudson.

Caitlin and John Matthews, *The Western Way*, Vols. I and II, Arkana, RKP.

Emily Peach, *The Tarot Workbook*, Aquarian, 1984.

Israel Regardie, *The Complete Golden Dawn*, Aquarian.
   The Middle Pillar, Aquarian.

Alan Richardson, *Introduction to the Mystical Qabalah*, Aquarian.
   Priestess (biography of Dion Fortune), Aquarian.

Starhawk, *The Spiral Dance*, Weiser, USA.

Doreen Valiente, *ABC of Witchcraft*, Hale.
   Natural Magic, Hale.
   Witchcraft for Tomorrow, Hale.

Tony Willis, *The Runic Workbook*, Aquarian.

Index